# Church Planting Is for Wimps

## Other 9Marks Books:

The Church and the Surprising Offense of God's Love
*Jonathan Leeman*

What Is a Healthy Church?
*Mark Dever*

What Is a Healthy Church Member?
*Thabiti M. Anyabwile*

The Gospel and Personal Evangelism
*Mark Dever*

What Does God Want of Us Anyway?
*Mark Dever*

What Is the Gospel?
*Greg Gilbert*

It Is Well
*Mark Dever and Michael Lawrence*

Biblical Theology in the Life of the Church
*Michael Lawrence*

# Church Planting Is for Wimps

How God Uses Messed-up People
to Plant Ordinary Churches
That Do Extraordinary Things

## Mike McKinley

Foreword by Darrin Patrick

CROSSWAY

WHEATON, ILLINOIS

For Karen,
God's gift to me on this journey

Trade paperback ISBN: 978-1-4335-1497-5
PDF ISBN: 978-1-4335-1498-2
Mobipocket ISBN: 978-1-4335-1499-9
ePub ISBN: 978-1-4335-2464-6

**Library of Congress Cataloging-in-Publication Data**
McKinley, Mike, 1975–
   Church planting is for wimps : how God uses messed-up
people to plant ordinary churches that do extraordinary
things / Mike McKinley
      p. cm. (A 9Marks book)
Includes bibliographical references and index.
   ISBN 13: 978-1-4335-1497-5 (tpb)
   ISBN 10: 1-4335-1497-4 (tpb)
   ISBN 10: (invalid) 1-4335-2464-6 (ebk)
   1. Church development, New. I. Title.
BV652.24.M37     2010
254'.1092—dc22            2009031789

Crossway is a publishing ministry of Good News Publishers.

| VP | | 19 | 18 | 17 | 16 | 15 | 14 | 13 | 12 | 11 | 10 |
|----|----|----|----|----|----|----|----|----|----|----|----|
| 14 | 13 | 12 | 11 | 10 | 9 | 8 | 7 | 6 | 5 | 4 | 3 | 2 | 1 |

# Contents

# Foreword

If you have watched the movie *Saving Private Ryan* you will never forget the opening scene. If you haven't seen it, the following list sums it up:

- Bullets flying.
- Blood flowing.
- Terror raging.
- Soldiers losing.

Some lost their limbs, some their lives, and some their sanity.

Church planting is not a physical war, but it is most definitely a spiritual war. In this spiritual conflict, just as in a physical battle, there are enemies, weaponry, danger, fear, and a lot of pain. But the way to win this spiritual war isn't by powering up and being a "tough guy," but by surrendering your will and becoming God's guy. Your city's battlefield doesn't require churches planted by men who are known as heroes. What we need today are churches planted by men who are known as humble.

Mike McKinley, as you are about to clearly perceive, is such a man. He is more impressed with Jesus than he is with himself, and serves as a trusted guide for those of us who are wading into terrifying waters or are in the midst of a full-blown church planting battle.

Mike shows us that you can plant a church that takes the Bible seriously and reaches diverse peoples, and that you don't have to chuck biblical faithfulness in order to preserve cultural relevancy. He boldly attempts to get us on the "faithfulness path" by getting us off the "numbers treadmill" that often plagues the church planting world. He also shows us that your church doesn't have to be lily white, even if it is planted in the soil of the suburbs.

Mike's book is not just a battle cry for the rallying of the troops. It also functions as a weapon to be added to every church planter's arsenal.

Darrin Patrick
Founding Pastor of The Journey,
St. Louis
Vice-President: Acts 29
Author of *Church Planter: The Man,
The Message, The Mission*

# Acknowledgments

I owe a lot of people a lot of thanks. Please allow me a moment to express my gratitude at the outset.

A great deal of thanks is owed to my friends at 9Marks. Jonathan Leeman has been both an excellent friend and an excellent editor. Matt Schmucker and Mark Dever have taught me the gospel in word and deed for fifteen years. I am very grateful to God for you all.

Many thanks are due to the brothers and sisters at Guilford Baptist Church, who are a source of true joy and encouragement to me. Special thanks are due to my friends Gail Smith, Tim Fanus, Paul and Lisa Emslie, and Aaron Pridmore for their partnership in the gospel work at Guilford. I also must draw attention to some of the long-time members of the church, particularly Nancy Higgs, Doris Jenkins, Lem Jordan, Sharon Brown, and Lee Thompson, who trusted God enough to hand their church over to a twenty-nine-year-old who didn't know what he was doing. Being your pastor is one of the greatest honors in my life.

Finally, I am grateful for the wonderful family with which God has blessed me. My in-laws, Virgil and Susie Andrews, have been far kinder to me than I plan to be to the man who steals away my only daughter. My brother and sister-in-law have been generous with their prayer and encouragement. I also owe great thanks to my parents, whose love and support I've never doubted.

Without my children, Kendall, Knox, Phineas, and Ebenezer, life would have far fewer adventures, smiles, and joys. Thanks for giving up "family fun day" for a season so that I could write this book.

And to Karen, whose love and service I do not deserve . . . words fail me. Thank you for everything.

# Introduction: Justify Your Existence

The history of my life will say to the world what it says to me—There is a loving God, who directs all things for the best.

**Hans Christian Andersen**

One online e-zine has a regular feature called "Justify Your Existence." The gist of the feature is this: they take a band that you probably haven't heard, and they put to them the supreme challenge. They ask the band to convince the readers that it's worthwhile to grant them a hearing.

Well, I am aware at the outset that I bear the same burden. You haven't heard of me. There's no obvious reason you'd want to read anything I have to say. I don't pastor a large church. Despite what my mom thinks, I am probably not destined to be a famous preacher or conference speaker. I don't have a particularly brilliant methodological insight that will transform your life or ministry. But maybe that's all okay. I am not writing this book to help you build a giant church or to advocate a technique that guarantees wild success.

## What's in This for You

Instead I want to share with you my story of planting a church (well, kind of planting a church . . . we'll get to that later). It's not a particularly original way to present this material, but I think it is appropriate, because Christians are people in the middle of God's story. The small victories and slow progress of the gospel in our lives and churches are actually spectacular evidence of God's grace and exactly the things that make up part of his wonderful story of redemption.

So I hope that my story overlaps with your story in a way that's encouraging and helps your ministry. I have learned that God uses messed-up people like me and you to plant churches that look utterly unremarkable to the world. The marvelous thing is that, in his kindness, God does amazing things through those churches. My hope is that my testimony to God's everyday amazing grace will

- inspire some people to become church planters,
- encourage others who are in the middle of the church planting journey,
- spur pastors of existing congregations to invest heavily in church planting,
- and give all church members a better sense of how they might love and pray for church planting teams, especially if God sends them on one.

It would be my joy if, by the time you are done reading this book, you're thinking, *If God can use this moron, surely he can use me as well!*

To that end, I'll make a deal with you: I'll be transparent about my failures and struggles, which are legion, if you promise to be amazed by God's kindness. Do we have a deal?

## The Quick Bio

First, what do you need to know about me? I was raised outside of Philadelphia, so I have anger issues. You would too if you were an Eagles fan. My parents were brought to Christ through a painful family experience when I was about nine or ten years old, and they began dragging my brother and me to a large evangelical church in our town. One Sunday God showed mercy to me by giving me ears to hear the gospel, and I turned from my sin and trusted in Christ.

Even though I was serious about my faith growing up, I had what people today kindly refer to as "issues." My grades were good, and I didn't get into trouble with girls or drugs, but my soul was a mess. I was proud and judgmental, pretty much convinced that everything and everyone else was idiotic. I was a jerk, and I didn't know it. Had someone told me, I wouldn't have listened. Let's face it, as long as teenagers in the church are not getting into trouble with girls or drugs, no one is going to bother them. So I was left to grow more proud and more angry at other people.

As I grew older, church fit me less and less. Instead I found an outlet for my anger in punk rock music. Punk rock music sees the stupidity of the world pretty clearly without trying to give meaningful answers, and it gave me a vocabulary for my dissatisfaction. I appreciated its honesty, so I adopted its look and attitude. Besides, I looked good with tattoos. And still do.

Suddenly I didn't feel like I fit in with most Christians. I didn't want to be a Republican. I didn't want to spend my whole life pursuing a big house and a car. And I didn't want to wear khakis. Though I loved Jesus, I decided that I didn't need to be like everyone else in order to follow him.

My college years took me to Washington DC. I thought I went there for an education, but God had two transforming experiences in store, neither of which had anything to do with my classes. First, I met my wife-to-be, Karen. Like me, she loved Jesus and punk rock, and still does. I knew right away that I would marry her, and as this story unfolds, you'll discover why she's the real hero of our saga.

The other transformative encounter was becoming a member at Capitol Hill Baptist Church (CHBC), pastored by Mark Dever. Even though a vast majority of the church were over seventy years old, they warmly welcomed the green-haired guy in the kilt and combat boots. CHBC quickly became my spiritual home. My soul flourished under Mark's preaching, pastoral care, and friendship. And God used Mark's work of revitalizing the church to spark my own love for the church.

After college, Karen and I were married and moved back to Philly so she could continue her education and before I would attend seminary full-time. To support us, I worked as a full-time cubicle jockey selling insurance for cell phones. And we started cranking out kids, which also brought its full-time demands. (To jump ahead in the story line, we now have four children—Kendall, Knox, Phineas, and Ebenezer. Just thinking about them makes me smile.)

When seminary wrapped up, the congregation at Capitol Hill Baptist asked me to come back to Washington to join the church staff as a planter. So we had another baby, Karen shaved her head as a graduation gift for me, and we moved back to DC. We spent a little over a year on staff at Capitol Hill Baptist and then planted a church called Guilford Baptist Church with seven other people thirty miles away in Sterling, Virginia. Actually, it would be more accurate to say that the seven of us went to reform a church called Guilford Fellowship that already had twelve members, but I'll explain all this as we go.

That, gentle reader, is how this all began.

# Church Planting— Slightly Preferable to Unemployment

Slums may well be breeding grounds of crime, but middle-class suburbs are incubators of apathy and delirium.

**Cyril Connolly**

By the spring of 2003 I was tired. Really tired. I was working forty hours a week as a manager for an insurance company. This involved talking to unhappy customers who cared a little too much about replacing their cell phones as well as supervising entry-level employees who were either impregnating or hitting one another. I was also taking a full load of classes at Westminster Theological Seminary in Philadelphia, driving back and forth from work to school a couple of times each day.

Every morning I was in the office by 6:30. Every evening, at the close of the workday, my wife Karen would meet me in the parking lot of my office building to hand over the baby. She then went to work as a nurse at the local hospital's emergency room, while I headed home to study. Add in renovations and repairs on a hundred-year-old house, and not much time was left for sleep.

## Want to Be a Guinea Pig?

So when my former pastor from Capitol Hill Baptist, Mark Dever, called one morning and asked me to meet him that day on the seminary campus, I felt reluctant. I was happy to meet with Mark, but doing so meant staying late at work. It also meant skipping my fifteen-minute afternoon nap, which was often the only thing lying between me and the abyss. But Mark has boundary issues and a way of getting what he wants, so later that day I chugged a jumbo-sized cup of gas station coffee and slumped down on a bench outside the seminary library, waiting for him to arrive.

When he did, we started with a few moments of chitchat, but he turned to business pretty quickly. Capitol Hill Baptist was growing out of its meeting space, he said, and the cost of making significant renovations to their old building was exorbitant. The elders of the church had decided to implement a strategy to plant churches in the surrounding suburbs. Mark was here to float a trial balloon: would I be interested in returning to DC after seminary to be CHBC's guinea pig church planter?

I would eventually say yes, of course. Mark is a made man in the Reformed Mafia. He has a giant Alliance of Confessing Evangelicals logo tattooed on his back. He has J. I. Packer's home phone number in his contact list under "Jim P." You don't say no to a guy like this.

But even if it wasn't Mark who was asking, the last seven years in the cell phone insurance biz left me willing to take a job as an assistant manager at Wendy's, the fast-food hamburger chain. In fact, I had tried, and they turned me down, but that's a tale for a different book. Since many of my seminary friends had spent three years and thousands of dollars on classes but were struggling to find a full-time ministry opportunity, I wasn't about to forfeit an opportunity like this. So I told him that I would talk to Karen, who I didn't think would be excited about moving, and get back to him.

## Planting for Hipsters

I had already received a few other offers to plant churches, but I had turned them down. I had never thought of myself as a church planter. Seminarians often talk about church planting as if it requires an indelible mark on the soul. "Are you a church planter?" they ask in hushed tones. The truly gifted men can recall thoughts of planting from their time in their mother's womb. I, on the other hand, had checked my soul twice but never found any indelible marks, at least not of that kind.

Still, several organizations had approached me about planting churches in the trendy part of the city where all of the wealthy young professionals live and drink. The idea, I think, was that I would be the tattooed pastor in the punk rock band T-shirt with a church full of twenty-somethings, all of whom wore plastic black eyeglasses. We would meet in a warehouse on Tuesday nights, followed by a trip to the local brew-house. Good theology. Loud music. Maybe a trendy church name taken from a Greek or Latin word that will sound cool for five or six years.

Can you see the picture? Let's face it—it would have been a lot of fun. I could have met cool people and done some good ministry.

But it seemed like a really bad way to build a church.

Don't get me wrong—I can see how such a scenario presents an effective way to draw a crowd. People favor people who favor them. They favor goods and services tailored to their tastes and how they want to perceive themselves. Niche marketing works. So plant a church that gives off an intelligent, slightly rebellious, funny, hipster vibe, and you will attract pre-wealthy twenty-somethings, since that's how they want to feel about themselves. If you do it artfully, you may attract lots of them. Hopefully you'll be able to help those twenty-somethings you've attracted: lead them to Christ, teach them a lot about Jesus, equip people to care for the city. I'm not knocking it. That would be great! But . . .

I don't think you would have a very *healthy* church. The Bible seems to assume that a church will express diversity in age. As just one example, think of Paul's instructions to his protégé Titus:

> But as for you, teach what accords with sound doctrine. Older men are to be sober-minded, dignified, self-controlled, sound in faith, in love, and in steadfastness. Older women likewise are to be reverent in behavior, not slanderers or slaves to much wine. They are to teach what is good, and so train the young women to love their husbands and children, to be self-controlled, pure, working at home, kind and submissive to their own husbands, that the word of God may not be reviled. Likewise, urge the younger men to be self-controlled. (Titus 2:1–6)

Here Paul has instructions for the old men (be temperate and worthy of respect) and the young men (be self-controlled). He even has things for the old women to teach the young women about how to be godly wives and mothers! It's hard to see how that happens if everyone in the church is the same age, right? Are the twenty-seven-year-olds supposed to teach the twenty-two-year olds how to be godly at that stage of their life? I don't know about you, but I was pretty pathetic when I was twenty-seven (full disclosure: I'm still pretty pathetic).

In fact, if you look at what the Bible says on this subject, you'll see that one of the glories of the gospel is that it reconciles people that could never be reconciled without it. In Ephesians 2, Paul describes the glorious display of God's wisdom in the church as different kinds of people come together (specifically, Jews and Gentiles). In John 13:35, Jesus tells us that the world will know we are his disciples because of our love for each other. But if we only hang out with people who are the same age, who like the same kind of music, and who share our taste and politics and preferences, how are we any different from the world? Doesn't every non-Christian you've ever known hang out with people who are just like him or her (Matt. 5:47)?

Love in the church should be at least partly inexplicable to the world. The elderly ladies at Capitol Hill Baptist who, in 1995, invited the guy with the stupid hair and safety pins in his face to their homes for lunch after church—*they* were displaying the riches of God's wisdom to the watching world. When a church looks diverse on the outside, it's often because the gospel is central. That's why you want to see churches filled with political liberals and conservatives, people wearing jeans and three-piece suits, men and women with white and brown and black skin, Christians old and young, friends tattooed and tattoo-deficient, and so on. Churches that aim at just one demographic ultimately work against that show of God's wisdom.

## Don't Say "Homogeneous Unit Principle"; Say "Contextualize"

Not many books or church leaders these days speak anymore about the homogeneous unit principle—appealing to one homogeneous group of people. Somewhere in the 1980s or 1990s church growth writers stopped using the phrase because they had heard enough complaining about it being biblically problematic. Still, they needed some way to target particular groups, so they began to speak in terms of "contextualization"—adapting yourself to a context. I don't want to totally knock the good people-sensitivities involved with contextualizing, but the evangelical fascination with the topic makes me wonder if it's just an updated version of the homogeneous unit principle: Pick your social demographic and appeal . . . I mean, contextualize to them.

When we start churches intentionally designed to appeal to a certain kind of person, we fail to heed the biblical mandate to become all things to *all people* (1 Cor. 9:22). It seems like many churches want to embrace the first phrase without the second. We want to become all things to some people. The problem is, becoming all things to some people—say, by rocking the tattoos and turning up the music—often keeps us from reaching all kinds of people. After all, wooing one demographic (for example, urban young people) often means alienating others (such as older people or foreigners).

It seems to me that Paul in 1 Corinthians 9 wasn't saying that he would mimic the people he was trying to reach, you know, with a ripped tunic and Doc Martens sandals. He was trying instead to remove unnecessary offense whenever possible. He wasn't telling them to sport goatees—he was telling them not to flaunt their Christian freedom in everyone's faces. He was encouraging the church to be sensitive to surrounding cultures, yes, but by being sacrificial in its love, willing to give up things it might not have preferred to give up. To this day, I enjoy punk rock. I *could* flaunt the tatts and plant a punk rock church that took its musical cues from Stiff Little Fingers and its attitude from the Clash. But how would this show love for the elderly women in my neighborhood, the same kind of elderly women who welcomed me to Capitol Hill Baptist? It seems like we should intentionally plant churches that will, as much as possible, welcome and engage people who are different and diverse with respect to age, gender, personality, and nationality.

But this hardly ever happens! According to one study, only 5 percent of Protestant congregations in America are multiracial churches (defined as a church with an ethnic mix where no more than 80 percent of the congregation is of one dominant group).[1] Let that sink in for a second. If you are planting a church in a rural county where 99 percent of the population belongs to one ethnic group, I can understand why your church is mono-ethnic. But if we're starting churches in cities and growing suburbs, locations with great diversity, shouldn't our churches reflect that diversity? It could be that our efforts to "engage the culture" have pigeon-holed us into reaching only one culture group.

Perhaps you're thinking, *But young people simply won't go to churches where the music is not tailored to them.* That may be partly true, but it's only true insofar as they've been in churches with no biblical vision for reaching *all people.* But what if pastors everywhere decided to stop capitulating to consumeristic demands? What if pastors taught church members to lay down their rights for the sake of people who are different? Pastor, are you afraid that if you try doing this, you might lose some of your market share?

So then, what should characterize a church plant that wants to reach people from all kinds of backgrounds? Well, it obviously needs to show intentional love to people from different cultures. People from other cultures will know pretty quickly whether they are welcomed or merely tolerated as a curiosity. In our church we try to be intentional about having members from other cultures involved in leading our corporate gatherings, whether through prayer, Bible reading, singing, or preaching. In addition 40 percent of our elder board is comprised of non-white non-Americans (and that's not including the lawyers, who should perhaps be their own ethnic group).

Also, the way that we order our gatherings can impact the

---

[1] Michael Emerson, *People of the Dream: Multiracial Congregations in the United States* (Princeton, NJ: Princeton University Press, 2006). For what it's worth, as of 2009 our congregation in Sterling is roughly 70 percent one dominant group.

way international believers feel. Many of the brothers and sisters in our congregation from other cultures were attracted by how similar our services are to the ones in their home countries. The music is different, sure. The way people dress is different, of course. Our services may be quieter or louder than what they're accustomed to. But Christians gathered in churches in Thailand, in South Africa, in Niger, in Guatemala all do the same things: they pray, sing, read the Bible, and listen to the Word being preached. The more we focus on doing those things, the more "at home" international brothers and sisters feel. The more we import movies and drama and pop culture into the church, the more specific and targeted our gatherings feel, and the less comfortable these brothers and sisters feel.

Now, I am not saying there can be no diversity in trendy churches. You can point to large homogeneous-unit-pursuing churches that are wonderfully diverse. That makes sense, because when the gospel is clearly taught, there should be that cross-cultural unity. But I do think that their diversity has occurred despite their pursuit of the homogeneous unit principle. <u>Thank God, the gospel can triumph over all kinds of pastoral stupidity, including mine.</u>  Still, as we think about planting churches, we need to look for ways to cultivate diversity rather than pursuing homogeneity.

## Dying to Self with Porsches and McMansions

Anyhow, sorry for the interruption. The preacher emerged. Let's get back to our story. Capitol Hill Baptist was inviting me to plant the kind of church I wanted to plant, but there was one thing about their offer that I didn't like: they wanted me to plant a church in the Washington DC suburbs of Northern Virginia, which in many ways is wealthy and sterile like the suburbs of Philadelphia where I grew up. Growing up in the land of Range Rovers and Saabs had turned me into a punk rocker. What might living there permanently do to me? To make matters worse, the county where they wanted to plant, Loudoun County, has the highest median household income of any county in America— over $107,000 per year. Fairfax County, next door, is in second place.

*This* wasn't where I had envisioned myself working. Maybe I wanted to go somewhere that looked more like me. I don't like the suburbs—I'm a city guy at heart. And Karen was raised nine thousand feet up in the Rocky Mountains. The suburbs struck us as combining the worst of the city (crowded and ugly) with the worst of the mountains (nothing going on, no arts and culture, little diversity). We had always told ourselves that we would go anyplace the Lord called us, even China, just not to the ranch house in the suburbs. We wanted to serve in a place where people were needy, where there was community rather than endless McMansions. So Loudoun County, with its malls and shopping centers, didn't fit our passions. In fact, a Ferrari/Porsche/ Lamborghini dealership sits just across the street from where I'm sitting right now. No joke.

But I'm pretty sure Jesus said something somewhere about picking up your cross in order to follow him. As far as crosses go, this one was pretty minor.

And I do think that too many church planters get bogged down with a clear burden for a specific place. I mean, maybe God did give you a burden for a certain geographical area. If so, far be it from me to tell you otherwise. But I know a lot of guys who say they have a "burden" when in reality what they have is a "personal preference" or "a level of comfort" with a certain location. So they reject all kinds of gospel opportunities because it doesn't fit with their "burden." But if God gives you an opportunity to plant a church in a place that has either Christians who need a church to proclaim the gospel to them or non-Christians who need a church to proclaim the gospel to them, you should think long and hard about it, even if it's not in a location you would prefer.

So even though Karen and I didn't want to live in the suburbs, we began to pray about it. I was a little excited about the opportunity of planting through Capitol Hill Baptist, but I struggled with feelings of guilt over the fact that we would not be going to a more challenging location. After all, urban ministry, in my mind, has always seemed more hard-core. There are opportunities in the city to help needy people, to bring the gospel to bear on broken families, to bring the gospel of reconciliation where ethnic tension exists. In my mind, urban pastors are like the Navy Seals. They can hold their heads high at union meetings. But in the suburbs, you have BMWs doing the Chik-fil-A drive-through and then pulling anonymously into the garage with an electric opener. Ministry here is like joining the Coast Guard. It counts as military service, but you can't brag to your friends about it.

One day I was whining to one of my Westminster professors, Manny Ortiz, about whether I should plant a church in the suburbs. Dr. Ortiz has forgotten more about church planting than I will ever know, and he's planted many churches among the poor and needy. I figured that he would be sympathetic to my feelings. After he listened to me complain, he spoke words that seem obvious in retrospect, but which I had entirely missed. He said, "Wherever there are rich people, there are poor people mowing their lawns and painting their houses. Go and find them if you want to help poor people." I was immediately convinced that I should shut up and go where the Lord was obviously calling us.

But I wasn't sure that Karen would be interested. After all, there were plenty of reasons to stay in Philadelphia: We were glad to be living near family. We had good friends. We were plugged in at our church. We were about to have another baby. We enjoyed the neighborhood in which we lived. And we were just finishing the process of gutting and redoing our house. We could probably have found a job at a local church that would pay the bills and give me experience in pastoral ministry. It didn't make a lot of sense to move at that time.

But as we prayed, the Lord made it clear that we should go. Karen, believe it or not, has the gift of knowing what we should do. I'm not sure where that falls on the map of spiritual gifts in Paul's letters, but there are times when God speaks to Karen (not audibly, or so she says) and just tells her what's going to happen. I can tell when God has spoken to her because she gets a settled conviction in her voice. This is a really useful gift to have (or to be married to), so I've learned to recognize and listen to it. When she came home one day and said, "I was praying, and I'm convinced that we have to go to DC," I knew what had happened. Before she was tentative and hesitant; now we were both clear. We were going to DC.

# 2

# So, How Exactly Does One Plant a Church?

One large question remained outstanding: how does one go about planting a church?

I didn't really know anything about church planting. It seemed pretty intimidating and more than a bit overwhelming. The good news was, I would first spend one or two years on staff at Capitol Hill Baptist Church in Washington DC. Among other things, I was to use that time learning more about the process of church planting.

That said, pretty early on in the process I received some discouraging counsel about the entire project from one particularly well-known pastor and author. This man had come through DC, and when he found out that we were planting a church he told us, "It won't work. No one will want to go to your church when they could just drive a few extra miles and hear Mark Dever preach." Thanks, friend, because I wasn't already intimidated by the thought of starting a church from scratch in a place where

I'd never been. Now I had a firm "vote of no confidence" from one of my heroes that I could look back on whenever times got rough. This was in addition to the fact that the housing provided by Capitol Hill Baptist had no cable TV hookup, which meant no ESPN. All this made for a rough transition.

## The Game Plan

After several months on the job, Mark and I spent a couple of days back up in Philadelphia brainstorming about church planting. It turns out that the smell of urine in the streets promotes clear thinking, so Philly was the perfect location. We put together a game plan,[1] which was roughly as follows:

1) I would begin meeting with members of CHBC who might be interested in church planting. Mark and I identified 107 members who either lived a good distance from the church and might like the prospect of a church plant in their area or members who were relatively mobile and might be willing to relocate (like young single people). We decided that it would be best not to tell people up front that I was meeting with them for the purpose of assessing their fitness and willingness to plant. Mark was particularly concerned that no one in the congregation should feel like the elders considered them disposable or expendable. So I began scheduling lunches and coffee with members of the church in order to hear their stories and build relationships.

2) I would meet with other church planters and pastors in the area where we were going to plant. At first there was some question about whether Karen and I would go to Northern Virginia or Southern Maryland; then we visited Southern Maryland, and the choice was clear. I then spent a good chunk of my weeks driving out to meet with these men in Northern Virginia, many of whom became my friends and colleagues in the ministry.

---

[1] See Appendix 1 for the actual document that we wrote and presented to the church elders.

If you are going to plant a church, meeting with other planters and pastors in the target area is an absolute must. They give you pure gold. They know the area, they've been through the ropes, and they have their finger on the spiritual pulse of the community. Each time I had such a meeting, I would ask about the story of their church, explain my situation, ask their advice and counsel, and pray with them.

3) I would become more involved in the public teaching at CHBC. If anyone was going to follow me in planting a church, they would need to be confident that I could teach God's Word capably. So the elders gave me the opportunity to teach a series of Wednesday night Bible studies on the Ten Commandments, to preach a month of sermons at Christmastime, and to teach systematic theology in the church's Core Seminars (which is what you call Sunday school when you're too cool to call it Sunday school like the rest of the Christian world does). The goal was to teach often enough to build credibility with the congregation. Eventually the members of the church would learn to trust my teaching and leadership, or so the thinking went.

If you'll allow me to digress for a second . . . As I reflect on Capitol Hill Baptist's offer to me, I am struck by how selfless a church must be to plant another church. The members of CHBC sank quite a bit of money into my salary and expenses but asked for relatively little in terms of service to the congregation itself. The other members of the staff allowed me to "bump" them from opportunities to teach and fill the pulpit, which is coin of the realm for church staff members. All of this speaks to the church's love for the growth of the gospel over the growth of their little kingdom. If you are the pastor of a church and you are looking to plant another church, I'd encourage you to support your church planters like CHBC supported me.

## The Pot of Gold

The long-term goal, the pot of gospel gold at the end of the church planting rainbow, was to start a gospel work about forty-five minutes outside the city. Why forty-five minutes away?

- We believed that a church planted farther away from the mother ship would have an easier time getting off the ground since there would be less "competition." Competition, generally, does not go well for the church plant.
- It serves the people who travel over an hour to attend Sunday services, which was somewhat common at Capitol Hill Baptist. Such people cannot be very involved in the life of a congregation, and so planting a church in their neighborhood improves their opportunity for congregational involvement.
- It also serves their evangelism since they can also more easily invite unbelieving family, coworkers, friends, and neighbors.
- We hoped that planting at this distance would open up precious space at CHBC for people who lived in its neighborhood. And CHBC would have another church toward which to point visitors from Northern Virginia.
- CHBC could increasingly become a church of people who lived closer to the church, aiding its own congregational life.

It was a win-win strategy.

## The Disadvantages of Planting a New Church

The last thing to determine was whether we would plant an altogether new church or have the planting team join an existing church in order to revitalize it. Church planting (starting a congregation from scratch) and church revitalizing (reviving the ministry of an almost dead church) share the same goal: raising up a faithful gospel witness where none exists. Both have a unique opportunity to grow by attracting people not currently attending a church and to bring fresh energy to the proclamation of the gospel in a particular community.

Though I absolutely believe that church planting is wonderful and oftentimes the only viable option, we pursued church revitalization. Let me present some of the advantages and disadvantages of both planting and revitalizing, starting with the disadvantages of planting a new church.

First, starting a new church can present significant logistical difficulties. Oftentimes new church plants must meet in a portable environment—a location where they need to bring their equipment in and out each week. This can be expensive. Rent often runs thousands of dollars per month, and the initial equipment outlay can run upwards of a hundred thousand dollars. That can be a prohibitive burden on a small gathering of people who don't have a long-standing commitment to the church. After all, you want your core group to spend its precious time doing the work of ministry—greeting visitors, showing hospitality, teaching children, evangelizing the neighborhoods. Setting up speakers and chairs can make you feel like you're doing something, but it's merely a means to the end.

Also, the process of setting up and tearing down chairs and audio equipment each week is tiring. When I was considering a new church plant, I met with one pastor whose church had been meeting in a school for a long time. He remarked how the church's energy was drained by the week-in, week-out loading and unloading of equipment. The problem is, land in Loudoun County runs between five hundred thousand and a million dollars per acre. Even if you can get the county to approve zoning for a church building (which almost never happens now, since churches don't provide any tax revenue from the land), a new church plant will need millions of dollars in order to build. So starting from scratch often means committing long-term to the grind of meeting in a location not your own. Obviously you don't need a building to have a church, but it's not for nothing that Christians for thousands of years have found it convenient to have buildings dedicated to holding their pews, chalices, and whatnot.

In addition, new churches often don't have a well-established method for dealing with administrative matters such as payroll, taxes, budgeting, and bookkeeping. For people who are gifted to teach but not to administrate, this can be a real challenge. Certainly this is true of me. It took us two years into our plant before someone figured out how to submit the necessary taxes on time. Church planting organizations will often help a planter with some of these tasks, but significant fees can be involved.

Another difficulty that comes with church planting is that new churches have to work to gain credibility in the community. New churches are new, obviously. That can have some benefits. People are sometimes attracted to new things, like the McRib. But it does mean that a church has no instant name recognition in a community. It usually takes significant time and money to gain a foothold in the community's memory. I know of one new church plant that receives about three calls a week from people asking if they are a cult (it could have something to do with the goofy, faux, postmodern name they chose). That's not the kind of response you want.

## The Advantages of Planting a New Church

On the other hand, new churches have distinct advantages. A new church has no personal baggage (though it will with enough time). There is no set way of doing things that stifles energetic and creative outreach. There's no institutional machine that needs to be fed, no programs that need to be served and maintained for the sake of the long-term members. Thus a mentor of mine once advised me, "Plant a new church. That way no one can ever oppose you by saying they were there before you were." There's truth in that statement. If you have a clear and unique way that you want to do church, it can be easier to start from scratch. You can do things the way you want to do them, and if people don't like it they will stay away. That can make your road as a pastor much smoother.

New churches can also do a good job of reaching new residents of a community. This is particularly strategic in locations where the population is growing or changing rapidly. Someone who is new in town may be more attracted to the ministry where he or she can get in on the ground floor and quickly become an important part of the church's life. In addition, existing churches aren't always socially flexible; they have difficulty accommodating shifting demographics and embracing different kinds of people. A new church might better adapt to people from different socioeconomic backgrounds.

So those are the drawbacks and benefits of starting a church from scratch.

## The Disadvantages of Revitalization

The difficulties that come with church revitalization are many. Most significantly, there's usually a good reason why the church needs to be revitalized. When I was considering the prospect of revitalizing Guilford Fellowship, I contacted one mentor who had attempted a similar work early in his career. He responded simply, "There's a reason the church is dead. Don't touch it."

He was correct. This particular church had died through no quirk of fate. It had experienced more than ten years of pastoral leadership that had wavered between poor and bizarre. One previous pastor had been caught "borrowing" his sermons off the Internet. Another pastor had apparently mimeographed a monthly church newsletter, the margins of which he illustrated in ballpoint pen with some of the more dragon-oriented events of the book of Revelation. There's no mystery why this church had fallen on hard times. Pastors who borrow sermons and spend precious daylight hours drawing dragons don't tend to grow healthy church members. There was much to overcome in order to move the church forward.

Whereas a new church planter can build from scratch, a revitalizer usually has to do some tearing down first. And this is not usually well received. If the church had wanted to do the things that healthy churches do, it wouldn't be dead. The members are going to kick. Often this involves a long, slow, painful process. That's why a number of my friends have joked from time to time that church planting is for wimps. There are challenges to setting up a new general store in a dusty cowboy town when none exists, to be sure. But the sheriff who has to ride in and clear out a town's trash before building starts—he's the real man.

Which brings us to another disadvantage of revitalizing. It's not easy to find a church that's interested in being revitalized. Often the church is dead or almost dead because the outlaws took control. They're not looking for a sheriff to come in and clean up their mess. Still, revitalizing is at least a possibility because a couple of the town's citizens want change, and they're asking for you to come. That is a hard—but not impossible—church to find.

In addition, while it's true that new churches sometimes suffer from a lack of name recognition in the community, you don't have to exercise much imagination to guess why that could be a good thing. The reputation of older churches often works against revitalization. Maybe the church is only known for some past moral scandal, or racism, or unfriendliness in the community. One church revitalizer found out that the only thing for which his church was known in the community was an unwise decision to tear down a historical landmark on their property thirty years ago. (But isn't all this an argument *for* revitalization?)

When I got to our congregation, some of my neighbors were familiar with the church and were excited that someone wanted to get it going again. But when I mentioned to most people in the community what I was doing, they would simply ask, "Is that church still open?" or "You mean the boarded-up church on the highway?" We were primarily known for the fact that church signs had fallen over and the windows were covered with black fiberglass, making it look abandoned.

## The Advantages of Revitalization

On the flip side, there are a number of strategic benefits to revitalizing a dead church. First, revitalizing provides a kingdom two-for-one. Like church plants, revitalization efforts establish a new gospel presence in a town, but they also remove a bad witness. People in Sterling, Virginia, no longer see our church like a billboard that reads, "Jesus and his people are irrelevant. Keep driving." Instead they increasingly see a lighthouse on the hill. They increasingly see a vibrant and dynamic witness for the Truth. Yes, it's harder to mosey into town on your horse to set up a new general store *while* playing sheriff, but doing so benefits everyone, both the kingdom and the onlooking world.

Also, church revitalization encourages the saints in the dead congregation. Dead churches are often populated by faithful believers who are deeply committed to their congregation. They have hung in through lean times. They have shown up Sunday after Sunday even though little was happening. These dear sheep are loved by the Savior, but they usually do not have a pastor who can care for them. When we were considering our options in Sterling, it seemed wrong to begin a new church in Guilford's backyard while the people there struggled.

When a church is revitalized, these saints are encouraged and shepherded in a new way. One of my chief joys as a pastor has been to hear some of the older women in our congregation recount stories of praying faithfully for this church for years. Now they are delighted by what God has done. Their faith is refreshed, and they are encouraged anew as they serve the growing body.

Finally, church revitalization enables us to harness resources for the gospel. Oftentimes dead churches are sitting on a treasure trove of resources (land, money, equipment) that can be leveraged for the spread of the gospel (Luke 16:9). Guilford Fellowship had a building. It had land worth millions of dollars. And it had over one hundred thousand dollars in the bank. All of those resources were just sitting around, doing almost nothing for the kingdom. Simply as a matter of good stewardship, evangelical churches interested in planting should consider revitalizing as well. Our work at Guilford has allowed us to leverage those resources to revitalize one church, plant another, evangelize our community, and support missions. If we had planted a new church instead, we would be broke, and Guilford's money would probably still be sitting in the bank.

## The Path We Chose

Is church planting for wimps? Well, planting and revitalizing take different kinds of courage, and God appoints a particular task for every man. Go where God guides you. As Karen and I thought about our future, we wanted to take the path of revitalizing an existing church even though we realized that the chances were slim that we would find such a church. I believe revitalizing may be more difficult at the outset, but I also believe that it offers all the rewards of planting—a new gospel witness—and more: it removes a bad witness in the neighborhood, it encourages the saints in the dead church, and it puts their material resources to work for the kingdom.

The question before us was, how would we find a church that was a good candidate for revitalization? As I said before, it's not like dead churches are beating down the doors seeking to be revitalized. The good news is, we serve a sovereign God who has a way of getting exactly what he wants. Sure enough, one day I walked into my office at CHBC and found something he had left on my desk.

# 3

# One Thing Is Necessary

And yet while I was asleep, or drinking
Wittenberg beer with my Philip Melanchthon
and Amsdorf, the Word inflicted greater injury
on popery than prince or emperor ever did.
I did nothing, the Word did every thing.

**Martin Luther**

There was terrible traffic on the Saturday we moved our belongings from Philly to Washington DC. I sat in an unending snake of cars on the Baltimore-Washington Parkway, and I began to feel doubt creeping into my thoughts. What was I doing? I didn't know anything about planting a church. How would we find a dying church with compatible theology that would welcome a revitalization effort? Would members of CHBC really want to follow me? A lot of unlikely things had to happen in order to get from this truck stuck in a traffic jam to someday pastoring a real church with people in it.

If I were a holier person, I probably would have reflected on Jesus' words, like "apart from me you can do nothing" (John 15:5) or "all authority in heaven and on earth has been given to me" (Matt. 28:18). As it was, I think I prayed something like, "God, if you want this to happen, you're going to have to do something dramatic." Then I turned up the radio.

## Before We Could Unpack

Karen and I finally arrived in DC, unloaded the truck, and spent a couple of weeks unpacking. But even before we were unpacked, God set the church planting wheels in motion. On my very first day in the office at CHBC, I found a memo on my desk from Mark Sherrid, a CHBC intern who was on his way to Louisville to attend Southern Seminary. Mark had been discipling a married couple at CBHC who had decided to move from DC to Northern Virginia. Since the couple was young in the faith, Mark decided to help them look for a good church near their home. So he printed off a list of Southern Baptist churches in their new hometown (Sterling, Virginia) and began to visit one each Sunday.

In the course of those visits, Mark came across a church named Guilford Fellowship. In his memo to me, he painted a picture of a church that was circling the drain. About twenty people attended on Sunday morning (a few weeks later another family would leave). The facilities were in poor condition. The previous pastor, apparently, had not done a good job leading the church and preaching the Word. There was no discernible leadership and no clear path forward. The church had received a large chunk of money from the state in an eminent domain case but had not been able to settle on a new pastor despite receiving hundreds of resumés.

Mark could not encourage a couple of new believers to attend such a church, but he did recognize the potential for revitalization. So he put me in touch with the church.

At first glance it all seemed providential. Here was exactly what

Karen and I were looking for—a struggling church with a building and with conservative theology. As an added bonus, Guilford Fellowship was in a perfect location, right off a major highway near Dulles Airport. I was excited, so I contacted one of the members of the church and arranged to preach for them on a coming Sunday and to meet afterward to explore future possibilities.

## Septic System Pump Trucks and Carousels

Sure enough, several weeks later Karen and I drove out to Guilford Fellowship on a Sunday morning with a few people from Capitol Hill Baptist. I had been imagining the possibilities and was excited that this little church might just be the answer to my pathetic, stuck-in-traffic, moving truck prayer . . .

And then we drove up to the church.

I am sure there were more depressing places on earth that day. Yet if we were to discount all those places where people were actually dying, it would have been hard to beat this little Baptist church that Sunday for its bleak languor, like a worm-eaten old cat sucking in its last few beleaguered breaths. Let me try to describe the scene for you.

First, the location was unsightly. The state of Virginia had built the main road directly behind the church; so the cinder-block rear of the church building looms over everyone passing by. Once we exited the main road onto the side road that takes you to the church, we found ourselves running a gauntlet of septic tank companies and down-on-their-luck kiddy amusement ride companies. Nothing says "wrong side of the tracks" better than septic pump trucks and creepy, peeling 1960s carousel horses. Let me put it this way: when a domestic beer distributor moved in across the road recently, it significantly upgraded the neighborhood's ambience. We then pulled into the church's gravel parking lot with no gravel but only knee-high weeds. A child-sized wooden cross was planted in the yard, guarding the front door menacingly. On the positive side, the church signs were weathered so badly that it was unlikely anyone would be able to identify which church this was.

Things didn't improve once we got inside the building. First, we walked into the two-story, cinder-block wing of the church built in the 1950s. This part had been redecorated in the 1980s, apparently when things like putting carpet on walls seemed like a good idea. The carpeting on the floor had come loose, forming large bumps and waves that threatened to trip senior citizens and small children. There were piles of clutter lying around, and decorations from previous years' Vacation Bible School still hung on the walls. The men's room looked like it had been decorated by the set designer from the horror movie *The Silence of the Lambs*. The carpet in the nursery area had an ominous brown stain, which went well with the cracked windows and mildewed walls. Crosses were scattered indiscriminately throughout the building, including one suspended from the ceiling at just the right height for someone to knock his head into it. Yellowing framed posters covered the walls (think "Footprints in the Sand").

We walked next into the main gathering place, which was a small 1870s chapel. The space itself was nice, with high ceilings and eight large, old windows. Unfortunately, someone had covered these windows with dark red fiberglass inserts, perhaps to make them look like stained glass. Yet the "stained glass" made the chapel look boarded-up from the outside and glow dark red on the inside, causing it to look just a little bit like hell. Of course, hell would not have six crosses strewn about the room, including one hanging behind the pulpit about a foot off-center, which was more visually annoying than you might imagine. Add to all this a display case full of Roman Catholic chalices and patens, overhead lights full of dead bugs, and 1970s wood paneling, and you had a building that was best renovated with a backhoe or even dynamite.

## An Ecclesiastical *Hindenburg*

The Sunday gathering fit the decor perfectly. Small churches tend to act like small churches, which is fine if you don't want anyone who is not part of your small church to ever become part of your small church. But if you do want visitors to come back to your church, having people in the pews call out prayer requests, song selections, and announcements isn't a great strategy. It's probably better to act as if you have thought in advance about what you are going to do in the meeting.

More striking, it looked as if a couple of the people weren't actually there to worship God. The kid running the projector kept putting jokes up on the screen in between songs, things like the words "Jim's head" with an arrow pointing to the head of the guy playing keyboard. (Though in retrospect, you have to give him credit; at least *someone* had thought about the meeting in advance.) Other people kept getting up and leaving in the middle of the service, only to return fifteen minutes later. When I stood up to preach, I saw that two teenagers were publicly displaying their affection in the back pew and continued to do so throughout the sermon.

The poor friends who had accompanied us from Capitol Hill Baptist weren't sure whether to laugh or cry. Mercifully, the service ended quickly, and we headed to the parking lot and got ready to return to Washington. I think that it was obvious to everyone: this was not the church for which we were looking.

To everyone, that is, except my wife. Right after Karen had finished sanitizing the children from head to toe with disinfectant wipes and buckling them into their car seats, she turned to me and said, "We are totally coming here to revitalize this church."

My stomach turned. I knew what this meant. As I mentioned earlier, when Karen knows what should happen, it happens. It might take months or years, but I knew that I would eventually figure out what she already knew.

But it clearly wasn't going to happen right away. I had little interest in being the captain of this tiny ecclesiastical *Hindenburg*. Plus, the timing wouldn't work. I had just arrived at CHBC and needed time to get pastoral experience and build a church-planting team, and Guilford wanted to hire a pastor right away. So we parted ways amicably. I offered to help them find people to fill their pulpit, they thanked me for coming, and we moved on with our lives and put the whole experience out of our minds.

## Becoming Their Pastor, After All

When I got back to work at Capitol Hill Baptist, I continued to fill my schedule by meeting with pastors and church planters in the area in order to pick their brains and get advice. As I asked questions, I began to realize that they all agreed on two things:

- It would be really nice to have a church building.
- Given the economic conditions and rapid growth rate in Loudoun County, no new church plant should ever expect to get a permanent building.

The county is very reluctant to rezone commercial lots for churches since they don't pay real estate taxes. Even if you can find an affordable piece of property in a good location with proper zoning, you'll still be competing against commercial real estate developers with much deeper pockets. Most church properties that are sold in Northern Virginia are converted into housing, office buildings, or retail shops. The only realistic hope for a building is to buy the property of an existing church that is closing or moving.

Suddenly Guilford Fellowship looked more attractive. After all, we could change everything that was wrong with it. Six months had passed, but I contacted one of the leaders at Guilford out of curiosity and learned that they still hadn't hired a pastor. Karen and I discussed and prayed over the matter, and we decided that the possibilities were worth the problems. So I restarted the conversation. I preached a few times for them, began to recruit a team from CHBC, and met with the whole Guilford congregation for an interview. We could all sit around one large table.

Now, frankly, I don't think anyone at Guilford Fellowship was excited about the prospect of me as their pastor. I was twenty-nine years old with no experience but a lot of opinions about how things should be done. Yet most of the congregation recognized that they had no other viable options. Anyone with a more attractive background would receive more attractive offers. Sadly, I was their best shot.

On the positive side, I was a package deal. CHBC would continue to pay the larger share of my salary for two years, and I would bring people with me to get the work going again.

Still, a couple of people at Guilford didn't like the sound of change, so they opposed the whole venture. Or maybe they just didn't like me personally, as unlikely as that seems. Either way the church finally managed on Sunday to bring the matter to a vote. And . . .

The vote didn't pass. Fourteen people were present for the vote. Ten voted to call me as pastor, and four abstained. Since the church constitution required a 75 percent threshold when calling a pastor, the abstentions counted as "no" votes. The whole thing was complicated by the fact that the church had no formal membership list. Could the teenagers vote? Or the old man who had attended for years but had never become a member? Or the lady who was a member but hadn't attended in a year but was brought in by the people who didn't like me? Whatever the answer, I received a phone call that Wednesday night telling me that the motion failed.

What happened next isn't entirely clear to me, and the details I have are secondhand. Another meeting was called to consider the matter. Apparently some of the godly older women in the church spoke up and rebuked the people who were "holding the church hostage." It seems they changed one person's mind in time for a second vote, which went forward and passed.

When it came time to leave Capitol Hill Baptist Church, seven members from CHBC agreed to come with us. We had two young couples with new babies, two single guys, and a single lady who moved out to Sterling to help with the work. I was to begin as the pastor of Guilford Fellowship on June 1, 2005.

On our first Sunday several weeks later, we changed the name back to its original name: Guilford Baptist. One of the older ladies thanked me. "All these years I felt like we were living a lie. We are a Baptist church; we should just call ourselves what we are," she said.

## Plumbing or Preaching?

Let me pause the story for a minute in order to ask you a question. If you put yourself in my shoes, what would you have said the greatest need at Guilford was on that day in June? Given the total disarray on almost every front, what one thing did the church need most? Surely, some things needed immediate attention.

Three of the four toilets in the church didn't work. Even Spurgeon couldn't grow a church if people cannot use the bathrooms. The signage needed to be addressed. It's tough to invite people to your church if they can't find it. The red fiberglass needed to come off, and the weeds in the parking lot needed to be cut. With all that, what would you say was the church's greatest need? What should be a church planter/revitalizer's highest priority?

Let me suggest an answer that may not be immediately apparent: the one thing that Guilford Fellowship needed most from its new pastor was to have God's Word preached in a clear, systematic, and compelling way.

Why? Because the Word of God stands at the center of the life of the church. As Edmund Clowney puts it, "The church is the community of the Word, the Word that reveals the plan and purpose of God. In the church, the gospel is preached, believed, obeyed. It is the pillar and ground of the truth because it holds fast to the Scriptures (Phil. 2:16)."[1] God's Word mediates God's presence to us.

Churches gather in order to know God and to be in his presence. And nowhere does the Bible say that we should seek or expect to know God through ecstatic visions, impressions on the soul, a prophetic word, or dreams. God may sovereignly choose to use such methods of communication from time to time. But the normal way that God speaks to show us what he's done, what he's like, and what he wants from us is through his Word. And God's church comes into contact with his Word through reading it, preaching it, and hearing it.

Listen to the apostle Paul's advice to a young pastor/church planter: "Until I come, devote yourself to the public reading of Scripture, to exhortation, to teaching" (1 Tim. 4:13).

Listen again to what he says to the same pastor/planter in another letter:

> I charge you in the presence of God and of Christ Jesus, who is to judge the living and the dead, and by his appearing and his kingdom: preach the word; be ready in season and out of season; reprove, rebuke, and exhort, with complete patience and teaching. (2 Tim. 4:1–2)

---

[1] Edmund Clowney, *The Church* (Downers Grove, IL: InterVarsity, 1995), 16.

Without God's Word, a church has no hope as it prepares to meet this God who is to judge the living and the dead. It has no way to know the gospel in a saving way (Rom. 10:14–17; 1 Cor. 1:21). It has no way to grow in Christ. Without the Word of God, a preacher, especially a young preacher with little history, has no true authority. He might be able to woo them with the devices of the flesh just like any comedian or rock star. But without the Word he will have no true spiritual trust from his people. Why would a church entrust its spiritual good to a know-nothing twenty-nine-year-old? Why would an older man who has been a Christian for twenty years, raised a family, and had a career care what this twenty-nine-year-old says about marriage or children or money or taking up your cross and following Jesus?

But if that twenty-nine-year-old can simply open the pages of the Bible and explain what God himself says, then the church has something with which to work. Then the authority rests not in the preacher or his personal wisdom and experience but in the authority of God himself who has breathed his Word.

Again, Edmund Clowney says it well:

> In every task of the church, the ministry of the Word of God is central. It is the Word that calls us to worship, addresses us in worship, teaches us how to worship and enables us to praise God and to encourage one another. By the Word we are given life and nurtured to maturity in Christ: the Word is the sword of the Spirit to correct us and the bread of the Spirit to feed us. In the mission of the church, it is the Word of God that calls the nations to the Lord: in the teaching of the Word we make disciples of the nations. The growth of the church is the growth of the Word (Acts 6:7, 12:24, 19:20): where there is a famine of the Word, no expertise in business administration or group dynamics will build Christ's church.[2]

---

[2]Ibid., 199–200.

What Guilford Fellowship needed most fundamentally was someone to preach God's Word to them. And, friend, if you are a church planter or church revitalizer, this is what your church needs as well.

## Three Enemies

If what I said about the centrality of God's Word is true, then why do we church leaders spend so much time doing other things? I want to suggest three things that keep church planters from focusing on their primary responsibility to preach God's Word.

### Misplaced Pragmatism

The first enemy of the priority of preaching is misplaced pragmatism. If you are a church planter or revitalizer, you might have the feeling on any given day, as I can, that teaching and preaching God's Word (or preparing to teach, which is far more time-consuming) doesn't seem like the most effective way to build and grow a church. It feels like your time would be much better spent evaluating marketing materials, meeting people, scouting out locations, planning children's programs, and fixing up the building.

In my first days at Guilford, I would cringe watching visitors come into the Main Hall on Sundays and look around at the chaos and dirt. I would come into the office each day and find myself enticed by a persistent temptation to skip sermon preparation in order to fix, clean, or remove something.

That's not to say that I didn't do all those things. I worked hard. I grabbed a pry bar and ripped off the red window covers. I replaced toilets, painted bathrooms, and put down new floors. I pulled weeds, dug out shrubs, and spread gravel. We organized work days and had people from Capitol Hill Baptist come out to haul trash, paint walls, and fix the parking lot. Eventually the building looked more like a decent and sanitary place to meet. Those things needed to be done, and no one else cared as much as I did (except, maybe, Karen).

But I did discipline myself to make sure that all this work was done during my overtime. Work on the building and the grounds occurred *after* taking care of my primary responsibility to prepare and teach God's Word. So, to be clear, I'm not saying that it's wrong for a planter/revitalizer to do things beside preaching. I am saying that preparing and preaching God's Word deserves our best time and energy.

In reality, *that's* the pragmatic thing to do if you want a healthy church. All of the other things seem more pressing and more important. It seems like designing attention-grabbing direct mail for the neighborhood or organizing a huge event would be the best way to build the church. But God tells us that his Word is the way he will build his church.

### Pride

The second enemy of making preaching a priority is pride. It requires humility to build the church on the preaching of God's Word, because it's not particularly glorifying to the preacher. But that's part of God's plan. As it turns out, he's actually not all that interested in your glory or mine. That's what Paul told the Corinthians:

> For the word of the cross is folly to those who are perishing, but to us who are being saved it is the power of God. For it is written, "I will destroy the wisdom of the wise, and the discernment of the discerning I will thwart." Where is the one who is wise? Where is the scribe? Where is the debater of this age? Has not God made foolish the wisdom of the world? For since, in the wisdom of God, the world did not know God through wisdom, it pleased God through the folly of what we preach to save those who believe. (1 Cor. 1:18–21)

Listen, if you preach a great series of topical sermons on marriage or finances or sex, your church plant might grow. If you are a savvy marketer and put up provocative billboards around town, your church might grow quickly. And people will think that you are great. You can wear trendy shirts, get blond tips in your hair, and wear a microphone that hooks around your ear.

But if you preach God's Word faithfully, few people will be tempted to think that you are great. If you stand up on Sunday morning and explain that when Jesus forgave the sins of the paralytic in Mark 2, he was claiming to be God and that the only way for sins to be forgiven was for God-in-the-flesh to take the punishment for our sins on himself on the cross, people will have one of two reactions: they will praise God, or they will think you are a complete idiot. That's the point. God has designed it to work this way. You preach and people get saved to God's glory, or their so-called "wisdom" is confounded and you look like a moron, also to God's glory.

### A Lack of Confidence in God's Word

The third enemy of the priority of preaching is a lack of confidence in God's Word. Right before I left Capitol Hill Baptist, I asked Mark Dever for a last piece of advice. He told me, "Do everything you can do to preach excellent sermons. Everything else will fall into place." I remember thinking, "That sounds right theologically, but will it actually *work*?"

Despite my misgivings I followed his advice since experience has taught me that Mark usually knows what he is talking about and I didn't have any other ideas. As it turns out, he was right. More accurately, God was right when he told us that he would give life through the preaching of his Word (Isa. 55:11; Ezek. 37:1–10; Rom. 4:17; 10:17; 2 Cor. 4:6; Heb. 1:3; James 1:21; 1 Pet. 1:23). That has certainly been our experience at Guilford. I began that first Sunday morning by preaching on Mark 1:1 ("The beginning of the gospel of Jesus Christ, the Son of God") to the dozen and a half people scattered around the room. I explained what Mark meant by using the word "gospel" and by calling Jesus "the Son of God."

I recently reread the manuscript from that sermon. It wasn't all that good, but it was true. Revival did not break out, but the sheep were fed.

For the first six months, I continued to plod along through Mark's Gospel, looking at what it teaches about Jesus' work and identity. Then I moved on to 1 Corinthians so the whole church could consider Paul's instructions to the church about unity and love. That seemed like a good thing to preach in the first year of a ministry.

As it turns out, choosing 1 Corinthians ended up feeling like a rookie mistake. The beginning of 1 Corinthians makes for great preaching to a new church. There are lots of opportunities to talk about the centrality of the cross, the importance of unity, and the priority of the local church. What I failed to consider was that 1 Corinthians also contains many chapters that are controversial and difficult. So it was difficult for some of the fifty people present at that point to hear three sermons in a row about Christian liberty. Those coming from a more fundamentalist background were being stretched significantly—or leaving—as we thought about all of the things that aren't essential to the faith. Then we moved into Paul's extended discussion of spiritual gifts, where those from a Reformed background had to come to grips with the fact that I am not a cessationist.

Still, rookie mistake or no, God used his Word. Those early sermons on Christian liberty, which in retrospect I might not have chosen to preach, had a huge effect in shaping our church culture. Though most of the people who initially came to our church wore a more conservative stripe (except the pastor), we didn't want to be a culturally conservative church. We learned from 1 Corinthians how Christians have freedom in Christ to make all kinds of different choices about what they eat, drink, listen to, and tattoo on themselves. As a result, when the church grew and less culturally conservative people began to come, there was genuine love and unity.

Since then, we have moved through Exodus and Ephesians, the Minor Prophets and Hebrews, and now the Gospel of Luke.[3] The church has grown both in number and in our understanding of the gospel. And we haven't grown because of programs, facilities, or advertising. We've grown because the one thing that Christians and non-Christians need is the Word of God. It is alive and powerful, and it's what our churches need. We should preach it with confidence that God will use it in whatever ways will glorify him most.

## Preach and Teach with Excellence

So, friend, if you are a church planter, give your time and energy to preaching and teaching God's Word with excellence. I'm not saying you should write a full sermon and preach it if there's no one to whom to preach. I'm not saying you should rock a forty-five-minute monologue with three other people in a living room. I'm simply saying to teach God's Word. Evangelize using God's Word. Disciple people using God's Word. And then, when you launch a public service, preach God's Word.

---

[3]In his surprisingly not-terrible book *Starting a New Church* (I am ready for the worst when I see Robert Schuller has commended a book on its back cover), Ralph Moore recommends preaching through Philippians, Acts, Romans, and 1 Corinthians in the first two years of the new church. I think that's a good plan but would recommend preaching the Old Testament as well.

# Cleaning Out
# the Sheaves

Shortly after I started at Guilford Baptist, I walked across the parking lot one afternoon to get the mail. It was a hot day, so I took a path that would take me through the most shade. Along the way, I passed by a car parked in our lot with a man napping inside. Being no stranger to the joys of the car-nap myself, I went by quietly and walked back using a different route to avoid disturbing him. The next day I noticed he was back. And the day after that. And the day after that. In fact, this guy showed up like clockwork every weekday at noon. He'd pull his car into the shade and sleep for close to an hour.

Since I was a newly minted church planter, naturally I was anxious to do the missional thing. That's why God put me in Sterling. So I started praying for an opportunity to meet this guy and maybe share Christ with him. One day when I looked out the window, I saw the car sleeper pull into the lot and actually get out of his car to get something from the trunk. I sprung into evangelistic action. I introduced myself to the man but didn't initially tell him I was the pastor of the church. His name was John, he worked on a surveying crew, and he liked to take a nap on his lunch break. He was not particularly pleasant. In fact, after about five minutes of conversation, it was pretty obvious that he was a racist, had recently spent time in jail, and, based on the smell, was a big fan of cheap bourbon.

After a few more minutes of small talk, I let John go back to his car to sleep. Before I left, I told him that I was the pastor of the church, that he was welcome to use the parking lot all he wanted, and that I hoped he would come by on Sunday for a church service. I wasn't expecting his reply: "Oh, yeah. I am a member of your church. I was baptized there when I was eight years old. Yup, I've been a member of Guilford for over thirty years."

So here was a man who hadn't been inside our church building or any other, he said, for decades. He didn't know there was a new pastor. He didn't even know the previous few pastors. It was pretty clear that he had absolutely no interest in attending a church service anytime in the near future. Still, he considered himself a member of Guilford in good standing. He drove by the church building each day and thought, *That's my church*. He chose to take a nap in this church's parking lot every day because he had a sense of connection to Guilford.

If this kind of conversation with John was an isolated incident, I might not think too much about it. But I started meeting more and more people around town who considered themselves members of Guilford—in the grocery store, in my neighborhood, at the gas station, and so on. All of them had stories about being baptized, or raising their children, or having a wedding at the church. And they all thought of themselves as somehow part of the church. But none of them had been involved in the life of the church for years. And I had no idea if they were Christians or not.

I had lots of questions. Did these people consider me their pastor? Hebrews 13:17 indicates that I will give an account to Jesus for the people in the church that I have shepherded. Were these people included? Did they take some kind of comfort from the fact that they were members at Guilford? Did they feel assured of their salvation because our church had their names on the rolls? We needed some way to help them know that they were *not* members at Guilford Baptist—they were not in any type of relationship with the congregation.

Besides the people who hadn't attended for years, I had questions about the status of people who had recently left. Of the ten or twelve people who regularly attended Guilford when we arrived, half of them stopped attending after a few months because they didn't like me or the changes that I had brought. Now, to be clear, the problem wasn't that they had left. Though I had personal concern for them, it was unlikely they were going to be part of any healthy changes at this particular local church. It didn't help anyone for them to sit in the services and stare daggers at me while I preached, walk out weeping in the middle of the service, or write letters to the entire congregation about my aberrant theology and asking for mercy from God for having ever voted to call me as pastor. All of which really happened. But though they had left, none had actually resigned their membership. In fact, only one couple (the letter writers) told me they were leaving.

So it wasn't clear what anyone's standing was. Could the one angry couple rally a bunch of old "members" to attend a business meeting and vote me out as pastor? Clearly something had to be done, not just for administrative purposes, but for unity's sake and for the sake of the church's witness.

## Membership Matters

You see, church membership is really important. Different churches practice membership in different ways. But whatever form it takes, it's essential to know who belongs and who doesn't. Who's accountable to whom? That might sound exclusionist, but it's meant to be clarifying. If Christians are supposed to be different from the world, and if the church is meant to be a group of Christians committed to each other for the glory of God, it's essential that we know who "we" are. The members of the church are supposed to care for each other and pray for each other. How can they do that if they don't know who "each other" is? The leaders of the church are supposed to care for the church. How can they do that if they don't know who "the church" is?

To begin the process of establishing a proper membership roll, I began looking through file cabinets, boxes of papers in the attic, and piles of junk around the building, hoping to find a list of people who were "members" of the church. All I found was a record of baptisms and membership transfers from the 1960s through the late 1980s. I also asked some of the long-term members of the church, but they couldn't remember if there ever had been a formal membership list.

The first challenge was to find some way to remove the non-attending "members" without making it seem like I was trying to seize control of the church. It's better to do nothing than to move too quickly and make people wrongly suspicious of your motives. I began the process of "cleaning the rolls" at a regularly scheduled members' meeting. It was attended by a few older members, along with roughly twenty-five people who had been voted into membership in the past few months. I proposed that it would be helpful to create a church membership list and that we had one good tool at our disposal for the task—the church's covenant. It wasn't ever used in the life of the congregation, but it was on the books, and it was pretty good.[1] The group decided that we would require anyone who wished to remain a member of the church to simply sign the church covenant and return it to

---

[1] If you are not familiar with church covenants, they are basically one-page statements outlining the commitments and responsibilities of being a church member.

the church office by the next meeting, which was scheduled for two months later.

After the meeting, I asked a couple of the older ladies who had been in the church for a long time to help compile a list of anyone who could conceivably consider himself or herself a member of the church, including the group who had recently left. We sent each of these people a letter explaining the congregation's decision and outlining the responsibilities of church membership.

Two months passed, and not one church covenant was returned by anyone not in regular attendance. We took the covenants that we had received and used them to create a membership list consisting of thirty-six names.

Now, I realize that creating a membership list may not seem monumental or important. After all, the end goal of church planting or revitalizing is not merely to impose administrative order where chaos once reigned. But doing this accomplished several important things. First, we defined in biblical terms what it means to be a church member. We now had a clear promise from every member to love and care for other people in the church. We could now expect members to pray for each other and treat each other with love and care. We could now hold people accountable to the commitment that they had made. We had something on which to build.

Second, we helped our witness to the surrounding community, as well as our witness to the members we removed. I fear what kind of witness all our non-attending "members" had had in their neighborhoods and families, all the while claiming to be part of the church formerly known as Guilford Fellowship. The people I had met in the parking lot and grocery store now knew that they were not members of the church—at least the ones who would give me their contact information. I happily followed up with some of those people and tried to evangelize them. But in the meantime it became clear to them that Guilford could not publicly endorse their relationship with Christ by keeping them on its rolls. Allowing them to feel some type of assurance in their relationship with God because they felt connected to Guilford was not showing love for them.

Third, the membership list gave legitimacy to the decisions of the congregation. Whereas before we wondered if certain people would find out later about a decision made in a members' meeting and object to it, now we knew who was and who wasn't supposed to be at those meetings making decisions. With that process out of the way, we were ready to begin reforming some of the other key documents that shaped the life of the church.

## Without a Vision Statement, the People Flourish

With the membership list established, the first document we worked on changing was the church's mission statement. As Aubrey Malphurs has written, "I believe that a major reason why 80 to 85 percent of churches in America are in trouble is because they don't have a clear compelling mission—they don't know where they're going or should be going. . . . A well focused mission statement provides a target on the wall for the archer and all else who might launch the ministry arrow."[2] Well, if that is true, then the key to Guilford's turnaround would seem to be a clear mission statement.

So we took the church's existing mission statement, which was:

> Guilford is committed to fulfilling all the functions of a good church, but we believe that our main mission is *to implant in the people of our society an applicable knowledge of the Scriptures.*

---

[2]Aubrey Malphurs, *Developing a Dynamic Mission for Your Ministry* (Grand Rapids: Kregel, 1998), 14.

- "Implant" —In other words, we want to see God's people get into God's Word and God's Word get into God's people.
- "Applicable Knowledge"—Our teaching emphasizes application, applying the Scriptures to our lives in today's world.
- "The People of Our Society"—We are beginning with the people of Sterling, then branching out to the Washington Area, the East Coast, and the rest of the world.

And we changed it to:

That's right, we changed our mission statement to nothing. We simply got rid of it.

Yet we realized that it wouldn't be enough to merely address the church's mission statement. The congregation also had a vision statement that was in desperate need of attention. After all, George Barna warns us, "Individuals and churches that are content to operate solely on the basis of their mission in life generally flounder because their perspective is too broad, too ill-defined. Those that focus on their vision as marching orders have a much higher chance of success because they establish more realistic priorities and because they are more likely to be people-centered."[3] So with that warning ringing in our ears, we took the church's vision statement, which was:

Building Up and Reaching Out
- To rely on the power of God.
- To encourage the equipping of believers for godliness and service through the teaching and preaching of God's Word and fellowship.
- To reach out to the surrounding communities to minister to their needs; preaching the Gospel of Jesus Christ and disciple [sic] those who become Christians. (James 2:14–18)

---

[3]George Barna, *The Power of Vision* (Ventura, CA: Regal Books 1993, n.p.).

And we changed it to:

Yes, we got rid of our vision statement as well, replacing it with nothing. Now, I know that almost every book on my shelves on church planting says that you have to start with a clear mission statement and/or vision statement. And I'm not saying there's anything necessarily wrong with having either. But they both seem so unnecessary. What good did our old vision statement do for the guy sleeping in the church parking lot? I understand the importance of clearly expressing our goals and purposes in order to achieve them. I am not sure why we need mantras and formal statements in order to make that a reality. Somehow the church survived for almost two thousand years before Malphurs and Barna told us we had to have them.

Here's what I mean. What if the New York Yankees wrote a mission statement? It would look like this: Our mission is to win the World Series every stinking year. And what if the Yankees wrote a vision statement? It would look like this: Our vision is to see a championship banner raised in the Bronx every April. And what if they wrote a statement of strategy? It would probably look like this: We want to score more runs than the other team in enough games to make the playoffs and eventually win the World Series.

Stupid, huh? Look, if you don't know what you're supposed to be doing as a church planter, if you need to write out a statement in order to remember that your church is supposed to evangelize the lost and help Christians grow in Christ, friend, you shouldn't be a church planter. How about casting vision the way Protestants have cast vision for the past five hundred years! Teach God's Word! Explain it to God's people, and tell them God's mission and vision and values and purpose and strategy for their life. Don't refer them back to some mantra that you make sure everyone in the congregation has memorized. Teach them what the Bible says about what it means to be a faithful Christian and a faithful church.

## Clarity in a World with Many Gospels

We continued our revisions to the church's documents by addressing the church's statement of faith.

A few years before I arrived, the church members had undertaken to write a new statement of faith on their own. And, well, let me just say that you should pretty much never write your own statement of faith. When the Westminster divines decided to write a statement of faith, they took 120 super-geniuses and locked them in a room for three years. Unless you have that kind of theological firepower, you might not want to wade into these waters. Seriously, if you put one apostrophe in the wrong place you have committed seven major heresies. Stick to something that has stood the test of time and proven itself to be orthodox.

But truth be told, the statement that the church formerly known as Guilford Fellowship had written was actually not that bad. They had cut and pasted from the Baptist Faith and Message (Southern Baptist Convention statement of faith) and a local seminary's doctrinal statement. So the wording was pretty clear. The problem is that associations and seminaries benefit from a level of doctrinal agreement that churches don't need. So Guilford's self-written statement contained specific statements about the premillennial return of Christ, the fact of creation in six literal twenty-four-hour days, and the universality of the flood in Noah's day. I'm not saying that I disagree with those ideas. I just don't believe Christians need to agree on them in order to coexist peacefully as a church. Members of the church should agree that the Bible is true, but they don't have to agree on what it means at every turn. A church can have premillennialists, postmillennialists, and amillennialists as members. It can have members who read Genesis as teaching a literal six-day creation and members who prefer the day-age approach to the creation narrative. None of those issues are central to the life of the church or the gospel. Nor are they necessary for making decisions.

We do need to agree on foundational matters like the gospel, the inerrancy of Scripture, the nature of the church, and justification by faith alone. You and I cannot be members of the same church if you hold to a different gospel, if you don't think the Bible is true and authoritative, or if you think that you need to earn your salvation by works. Churches also need to agree on basic matters of polity, like baptism, so that we don't have to argue every time Mr. and Mrs. Jones bring newly born Junior to be baptized—should we baptize him or not?

So I chose the New Hampshire Confession of Faith (1833), a Baptist confession that had stood the test of time and has been used effectively by many churches. I announced to the congregation that we would be considering a new statement of faith and began teaching through the confession in our adult Sunday school, word by word and phrase by phrase. After about six months and several public meetings to discuss and ask questions about the content of the confession, the church voted unanimously to adopt it as the official statement of faith.

Again, I understand that most church planters don't become planters because they have a burning desire to teach through old confessional documents. But having a clear statement of faith is important, whether you are starting a church from scratch or revitalizing an existing congregation. Why? Let me cite five reasons:

1) The authors of the New Testament were both *clear* and *inflexible* about matters of doctrine. We should do all we can to

articulate and affirm doctrine, lest we stray from it. Paul tells us to watch our doctrine and life carefully (1 Tim. 4:16).

2) Having a clear statement at the beginning builds unity in the church. We want our unity to be based on a common understanding of the truth (cf. John 17:15–21). If you throw open the doors of the church to anyone coming in when you first plant, good luck trying to get any kind of doctrinal agreement once the church has grown. Instead we should make it clear up front what the church believes and what members are expected to believe as well.

3) Having a clear statement at the beginning promotes clarity about the gospel. In a world with a million false ideas about Jesus and a million false versions of the gospel, churches need to be clear about our very source of life.

4) Having that statement at the beginning helps protect the new church from the inevitable crew of crazy, heterodox, and divisive wolves that will regard your young, cement-is-still-wet church as an opportunity to finally shape the church of their dreams. So when the more-Reformed-than-Calvin guy offers to "mentor" you or when the more-charismatic-than-the-Holy Spirit guy tells you that God has told him to "encourage" you, you can point to the statement of faith and repel their attempts to remake the church after their image. The statement of faith, in that sense, works well as a shepherd's crook for smacking wolves.

5) Having the doctrinal statement in place allows conscientious Christians to opt out early if they realize they are not a good doctrinal fit with the church. Why did we change the name of the church from Guilford Fellowship back to Guilford Baptist Church? Well, you know, we are actually a Baptist church. People were going to find out our dirty little secret eventually, even if we gave our church some goofy,

vaguely numinous name. We figured we might as well be up front with it.

## Constitution and By-laws . . . I'm Serious

The last church documents I wanted to consider overhauling were the constitution and by-laws. The constitution and by-laws of a church are the governing documents that outline the church leadership structure and how the congregation will make certain decisions.

Now, look, I'll be the first to admit that I don't care at all about many of the issues addressed in the by-laws. I don't care if we should require a simple majority (one-half) or some type of super-majority (two-thirds or three-quarters) to pass an amendment to the church budget. I don't care if two or three weeks' notice is required to call a special members' meeting. I'm glad there are people who care (in my experience, mostly lawyers), but I just don't.

What I do care about is the nature and structure of the church leadership. And if you don't, you should. How you structure your leadership directly impacts the discipleship and spiritual livelihood of saints. In fact, I'd even say that bad leadership structures played a significant role in the decline of Guilford Fellowship's spiritual health over the previous several decades.

It was clear that Guilford needed to make drastic changes to its constitution. The church leadership structure that I inherited was a mess. Like most Baptist churches, the congregation was led by the board of deacons, which the old constitution called "the shepherding arm of the church." This was problematic for two reasons. First, the Scriptures assign shepherding duties to elders, not to deacons. Second, it led the church into self-contradiction and confusion. On one hand, the congregation had concluded years before that the Bible taught that women could serve the congregation in the office of deacon, a conclusion with which I happen to agree. But on the other hand, they concluded a year before I arrived that women should not be shepherds or leaders in the church, also a conclusion with which I happen to agree. The problem, of course, was that the constitution didn't call the deacons to serve as deacons but as "the shepherding arm of the church." So the women were allowed to be deacons, but they weren't allowed to shepherd, which is what the constitution said deacons were supposed to do.

As a result of the confusion, there were no deacons serving in the church when I arrived. The term of the previous three deacons had expired, and the church was not able to choose new leaders. Do I need to explain to you why that is not good for church health?

In addition, the church had followed the time-honored Baptist tradition of hard-wiring committees into the constitution. Committees, after all, were the cutting-edge church management theory in the early twentieth century when Guilford was forming. By 2004, Guilford Fellowship had six committees or commissions (evangelism, education, youth ministry, administration, fellowship, and worship), each of which required a number of positions (president, vice president, secretary, etc.), as well as a church council with seven lay ministers (the function of the church council was "to lead the church body toward its goals." Umm, can you be more specific?). Between the various commissions and the church council, several dozen positions needed to be filled. The problem, of course, was that only a dozen people were attending when I first showed up. What did this mean practically? It meant they had given up following their constitution and by-laws.

## Wanted: Fellow Elders

In place of all of that, I wanted elders who would function as elders by shepherding and teaching the congregation; and I wanted deacons who would function as deacons by serving the congregation and making sure needs are met.[4] I had let the older members of Guilford know about my desires before they called me as their pastor, and everyone who had an opinion on the matter agreed that it was a good idea.

But I didn't move on the issue at all for the first year, because I wanted to make sure that the church was ready. Therefore, I made sure to teach on the topic of elders before making any formal moves. In the course of my normal expositional preaching, I simply highlighted the places where Scripture spoke of churches as having elders. In Sunday school, I taught a class on what the Bible says about church leadership.

After the membership role was established, the statement of faith was in place, and the dust from both of these changes had settled, Guilford formed a committee to rewrite the constitution and by-laws with an eye toward establishing the biblical offices and streamlining the church's processes and procedures. That committee—wisely—decided that Capitol Hill Baptist had already invented this wheel; so we took their constitution, made a few changes, and presented it to the congregation. After a few months of fairly unremarkable conversation, the congregation, now seventy-five people, voted to adopt the new constitution. A few months later I nominated two men to serve alongside me as elders. Two months after their nominations, the congregation affirmed these two men, and Guilford Baptist now had a plurality of elders. In the two and a half years

---

[4]For more information on how elders and deacons should function in the life of a church, take a look at Mark Dever's *Nine Marks of a Healthy Church* (Wheaton, IL: Crossway Books, 2004), particularly #9.

since that time, we have added two more men for a total of five elders (myself included).

Again, all this talk of constitutions and elders probably seems out of place in a book about church planting and revitalization. Why make a priority of establishing a plural eldership, especially with a small church and so many pressing concerns?

Well, there's no reason that establishing a plural eldership necessarily means neglecting other important parts of the Christian mission. It's not *that* time-consuming. And to be clear, I'm not saying that establishing a plurality of elders is a hill to die on or an issue worth blowing your church up over. Better to wait ten years than to do it too quickly and damage the church. As Pastor Phil Newton rightly put it, "The goal of a church should not be to establish plural eldership at any cost, but rather to elevate the standards of spiritual leadership in the church at any cost."[5]

Yet I do think that many pastors and church planters underestimate the importance and benefit of having plural eldership. The New Testament always speaks of elders in the plural, and their presence in a congregation was so important to Paul that he left Titus behind in Crete in order to appoint elders (plural) in every town (Titus 1:5). Paul charged the elders of the church at Ephesus to guard and teach the congregation (Acts 20:17–38). And Peter warned fellow elders to shepherd the flock well by exercising oversight with gentleness (1 Pet. 5:1–3).

A church that wants to grow strong and healthy should also want gifted men who will exercise this kind of pastoral care for them. Establishing a plural eldership doesn't mean neglecting other important parts of the Christian mission; it means raising up more men to lead in the very work of Christian mission.

---

[5]Phil Newton, *Elders in Congregational Life* (Grand Rapids: Kregel, 2005), 56.

In fact, if I were to plant or revitalize another church, I would be very reluctant to do so unless I had another elder or two coming with me. I realize that bringing someone with you can be tricky, especially if you're moving into a small church that needs reform. But the one thing that Karen and I found to be especially difficult about the first year or two at Guilford was the sense of being alone in the ministry. Sure, as time went on there were many good people at the church, and we had brought a team of people with us from Capitol Hill who faithfully served. Yet no one else was an acknowledged leader. No one else was recognized by the congregation as called by God to bear the burdens of leadership. There were no others on whom we could place a burden without feeling like we were inconveniencing them. We desperately needed someone who would refer to the church leadership as "we," not "you." This sense of aloneness led Karen and me to the edge of burnout (more on that later).

Yet once we had elders, that dynamic began to change. Suddenly I had a recognized group of men (older men, wiser men) with whom I could deliberate about the affairs of the church. The burden of making decisions, planning strategies, and shepherding the flock was now spread across three sets of shoulders.

## Conclusion

All told, we spent about a year and a half cleaning up the church's organizing documents. That's not particularly exciting stuff, I know. But then again, most of the important things in life aren't exciting (a couple more examples off the top of my head: seat belts, antibiotics, and cement foundations). By establishing a clear membership list, adopting a concise and solid statement of faith, and establishing biblical leadership, we had laid the groundwork for the church to carry out its mission in healthy ways.

If you are planting a church from scratch, your path will probably look different. Maybe you will begin with a statement of faith (again, don't build on implicit agreement!) and only then move to constitute the church, establish members, and appoint officers. But realize that you have a great opportunity to reverse engineer your church. You get to start with a clear understanding of what God's Word says about church structures. Do you have the picture in your head? Now begin working toward that goal. Use the intervening time to teach your people well, to explain the importance of committing to each other and the importance of good church leadership.

# 5

# God Always Gets His Way

In 2004, when the members of the church formerly known as Guilford Fellowship were still looking for a pastor, they called the local Baptist association for help. The association dispatched a consultant who met with the church, learned about its history, and talked to the congregation about its hopes.

After taking time to assess Guilford's future prospects, the consultant, also a pastor and church planter in the area, met with the congregation a second time and presented his conclusions. He said that the church had two good options. They could shut Guilford down completely and allow a Spanish-speaking church plant to have the building. Or they could restart the church. This latter option would mean closing the doors for six months and then reopening it with a new name and none of the existing members in leadership. In other words, let the local Baptist association plant a new church in your building, and the plant will let you attend its services.

In light of Guilford's circumstances, I honestly believe that both of these suggestions were reasonable. But the idea of giving the building to a Spanish-speaking church was a particularly good idea. While official statistics indicate that about 15 percent of Sterling's population speak Spanish in their homes, the number is much higher in the run-down neighborhood of Sterling where my church is located. Not only that, official government statistics probably underestimate the number of Spanish speakers. Illegal immigrants make it a point not to show up on such reports. If you're looking for the real demographics of an area, the teachers and administrators of the local public schools are a gold mine. They live in the neighborhoods, they care about the community, and they actually know the people and not just the census data. According to the public elementary school down the street from our church building, 61 percent of the children in the school speak Spanish at home. Many of those children speak no English at all.

As this church consultant correctly surmised, the area greatly needed more Spanish-speaking churches. It's not that no churches conduct services in Spanish; it's just that most of them are either Roman Catholic or Pentecostal churches that have abandoned the gospel. A few English-speaking evangelical churches have begun side ministries for Spanish speakers. Local Baptist groups have started some evangelistic Bible studies. But there were not many actual churches preaching the gospel in Spanish.

For whatever reason, Guilford Fellowship chose not to disband and hand the building over to a Spanish ministry. This left them two options: close down completely or call me as a pastor. Apparently they chose the lesser of two evils and called me.

That said, the logic of a Spanish ministry became clear to me as soon as I took over the church. We were in a great position to reach the many very poor, unevangelized, illegal immigrants in the area. There was only one problem: no one on our church planting team was able to speak any Spanish beyond the menu at Taco Bell.

So I began to pray. Honestly, I didn't have much faith that anything would happen; it was more like preemptive blame assignation. Still, I reminded the Lord that I would be happy to help evangelize Sterling's Spanish-speaking population, but it would require something extraordinary on his end first.

And, as he likes to do, God did something extraordinary. A few months after I began the work at Guilford, a married couple from Capitol Hill Baptist who lived right down the street from our church building decided to join us at Guilford Baptist. The best part, though, was that they were both native Spanish speakers. The husband, Heriberto, is from Venezuela; the wife, Neissy, is from Guatemala. They are good friends now and still serve faithfully in the church, but at the time I didn't know them very well. One night we were having dinner at their house, and I mentioned to Heriberto that I noticed there were a lot of Spanish speakers in the neighborhood. I pointed out that no one at the church spoke Spanish except Neissy and himself, and I asked if he would pray about how God might use them to help our church reach Spanish speakers. At the end of the evening, they had agreed to pray about it.

Little did I know what God would do. It turned out that Heriberto is a gifted teacher and evangelist, which was unknown to me and, I think, to him. Within a few weeks he had begun an evangelistic Bible study for his neighbors and some of the men who worked for his contracting company. The group soon grew to twelve to fifteen people and started to meet in the church building on Saturday nights, a time that Heriberto used to teach through the Bible, book by book. After about six months several people had come to Christ. The members of Guilford Baptist were excited. We began to pray and help Heriberto in any way we could, like teaching ESL (English as a second language).

## Something Has to Be Done

As time went by, it became clear that we would have to do something for these new Spanish-speaking believers. We didn't want them simply to come to Christ and then float in space. The Saturday night Bible study was excellent, but it wasn't a church. There were no elders, no members, no discipline, no baptism or Lord's Supper. Bible studies are great, but they are not churches.

Every Christian should be part of a specific local congregation. As Steve Timmis and Tim Chester write, "To be a Christian is, by definition, to be part of the community of God's people. To be united with Christ is to be part of his body. The assumption of the New Testament is that this always finds expression in commitment to a local church."[1] To be a Christian means to be saved *from* something (sin, God's wrath, death, separation, enmity with God and fellow man) and to be saved *unto* something (worship, holiness, newness of life for all eternity, community, reconciliation with God and fellow man). It is not merely God's plan to save an isolated group of individuals; he is about the business of saving a people for himself. "Once you were not a people, but now you are God's people" (1 Pet. 2:10).

We the saints are a people! And God intends for every member of his one heavenly people to be part of a local church on earth—like embassies or outposts of that heavenly people. Guilford Baptist therefore wanted these Spanish-speaking brothers and sisters to know all the blessings of belonging to such an embassy or outpost for God's one people.

After investigating our options, it became clear that the best plan of action going forward was for us to begin a new Spanish-speaking church. We floated the idea of Heriberto cutting back on his company's workload in order to focus his energies on church

---

[1]Steve Timmis and Tim Chester, *Total Church* (Nottingham, UK: Inter-Varsity Press, 2007), 85. This book is also available from Crossway.

planting, but it didn't seem like that was God's call on his life. His business was a blessing to a lot of people who needed jobs, and it was an unending source of evangelistic contacts. To remove him from such work seemed counterproductive.

So we were again at a crossroads. God had answered our prayers and helped us reach Spanish speakers. But we needed him to do something else extraordinary in order to start a proper church for them. Little did we know what God would do.

One day, quite out of the blue, a friend from Capitol Hill Baptist called. He had heard about our Spanish group and had called to tell me that a couple named Fredy and Marta Hernandez was moving to America and was waiting to see what God might be calling them to do. I had never met Fredy or Marta, but I had heard of them. Fredy was the experienced pastor of a church in El Salvador who had taken a six-month sabbatical to come to the United States and do an internship at Capitol Hill Baptist. Now, in God's mysterious timing, their immigration papers had come through, and they were moving to America permanently.

I got on the phone and talked to Fredy, which was no easy task since neither of us are native speakers of the other's language. But somehow we muddled through the conversation and agreed to talk more when they arrived in DC. Eventually Karen and I met with Fredy and Marta and explained the situation, the need, and the great opportunities for the gospel. We also explained to them that we had almost no money to help support Fredy, but we did have a family who was offering to let them live rent-free in their basement. Talk about a great deal: "Fredy, we have nothing here for you—nothing to pay you, no church to pastor. But there are Spanish-speaking non-Christians everywhere, and we'll let you live in a basement!"

Even though they could have easily taken a job with an established Spanish-speaking church in Texas or California, they decided to come to Guilford. We held a big welcome dinner at the church, and Fredy came on board as a church planter in the spring of 2006. He began working with Heriberto's group, and the Lord began to do amazing things.

## Please, Jesus, I Don't Want to Be Jim Elliot

The very first day that Fredy was "on the job," he, Marta, and I sat in the church office praying. We didn't know what else to do, so we were asking God to do something marvelous. I specifically recall asking God to move in such a dramatic way that we could not help but see his hand at work. Not five minutes later a man walked into the church. Now, as I've described for you in a previous chapter, the church is not in a location that gets a lot of foot traffic. No one ever walks into our church building. But on this particular day a man walked in, obviously looking for something. I greeted him and offered to help him, but it quickly became apparent that he didn't speak any English. Had he shown up the day before, I wouldn't have been able to help him. But I ran and grabbed Fredy to come and speak with him.

It turns out that someone had told this man, named Salvador, that there was a place on our street where he could rent a hall for his girlfriend's baby shower. He hadn't been able to find it, probably because it doesn't exist, so he stepped into the church to ask for directions. Fredy spoke to him and explained that he had been misinformed, but he offered to allow him to use our church building for free.

It turns out that Salvador was a former member of Mara Salvatrucha (aka MS-13), an extremely violent street gang that runs drugs and kills people from Los Angeles to Washington DC. From what I understand, not many former members of the gang exist since almost everyone who leaves the gang does so via a jail cell or a cemetery plot. But here he was, wanting to throw a baby shower and grateful for the opportunity to use our church building.

A couple of months later, seventy-five Spanish speakers showed up for a baby shower in our church basement. I pulled up to the church while the party was happening and parked my car in the lot among all their cars and trucks. The men, complete with bandannas and gang tats, were outside drinking since we had asked them not to bring alcohol into the building. As I walked by, I waved and said hello, trying not to look scared and praying furiously that God would save them in some way that didn't involve me dying like Jim Elliot. On my way into the church building I bumped into Fredy. He was holding a Bible and had stopped at the doors of the church to steel his courage.

Well, Fredy went out and preached the gospel to those gang members. I don't know if any of them have become Christians, but over the years Fredy and Marta have ministered repeatedly to Salvador and his family and friends. Who knows what the Lord has done and will ultimately do with their labors! We could tell many similar stories of God's extraordinary way of bringing people into contact with the gospel through his church.

Now, to be clear, barring an unforeseen act of God, the new Spanish-speaking church (now called Iglesia Bautista Guilford Mision Hispana) will never be huge or even self-supporting. They are reaching an impoverished and highly transient community. One immigration raid at Dulles Airport deported almost 25 percent of the church. I'm not a church growth expert, but I am pretty sure that it's hard to build a giant congregation among people who are statistically likely to be deported by INS. Yet through that little church the gospel has been proclaimed not only to some hard-working, honest, middle-class Spanish speakers but also to alcoholics, prison inmates, violent offenders, and prostitutes.

## Low-hanging Fruit

The Bible teaches that the gospel will find its warmest welcome among the poor and destitute, the outcasts and the downtrodden. The riches of the world powerfully tempt us to trust in them for our well-being. That's why Jesus says that it's easier for a camel to go through the eye of a needle than for a rich man to enter the kingdom of God (Luke 18:25). It's not impossible to be materially wealthy and poor in spirit, but the materially disadvantaged have a spiritual advantage over those of us with the means to anesthetize ourselves from suffering and need.

This dynamic was true in the apostolic church. In 1 Corinthians 1:26–29 Paul writes:

> For consider your calling, brothers: not many of you were wise according to worldly standards, not many were powerful, not many were of noble birth. But God chose what is foolish in the world to shame the wise; God chose what is weak in the world to shame the strong; God chose what is low and despised in the world, even things that are not, to bring to nothing things that are, so that no human being might boast in the presence of God.

The Corinthian church was made up of weak and foolish people. God is not a respecter of persons, and he delights in saving the weak and poor.

That dynamic has also been true in the life and ministry of Guilford Baptist Church. I've been at Guilford for almost four years as I sit here writing. In that time we have shared the gospel with many English-speaking people, most of them middle-class or wealthy. We have been clear with the gospel, creative with the gospel, and faithful to pray for conversions. But God in his wisdom has blessed us with only a handful of new believers. The Spanish church has fewer material resources and fewer people, but they have seen ten times as many people come to Christ. To be clear, I think the faithful witness of both churches is pleasing to God (though obviously neither church is perfect). But the gospel has taken root in a remarkable way among the illegal immigrants and the poor.

When we moved to Sterling, Karen and I rented a townhouse on the other side of town. It was in an upper-middle-class neighborhood where everyone enjoyed a good job, spoke clear English, and had a college degree. But no one wanted to get to know anyone else in the neighborhood. People would come home from work in their fancy sedans, remotely open the garage door, pull into their garage, and close the door behind them with nary a hello to anyone. One day shortly after we moved in, Karen went door-to-door to introduce herself and invite people over to dinner. They all fidgeted nervously in their doorways as if she were a serial killer casing their house.

After a year at Guilford we moved our family closer to the church. We found an older neighborhood with a high percentage of Spanish speakers, and we bought a profoundly ugly house. (I spent last weekend tearing off the siding and drywall on one side of the house to get to the mold.) It was not nearly as nice as what we were living in before, but it had an apartment attached to it where Fredy and Marta could live and minister to Spanish speakers. We have now lived there for almost three years and have experienced many more opportunities to evangelize and minister to our neighborhood.

So if you are planning on planting a church, consider swinging at the low-hanging fruit, as one of my seminary professors put it. Think about ways that your church can reach out to those whose station in life might make them more aware of their need for Christ. Consider making your housing choices accordingly, even if it means living in conditions that might not excite your mother-in-law.

## A Display of God's Glory

One thing that I have particularly learned by being involved with the Spanish church plant is the evangelistic power of the church's love. Though only a handful of the members of Guilford Baptist actually speak Spanish, the church has been able to have a wonderful witness to Spanish speakers by showing them love.

There are serious tensions between the English-speaking and the Spanish-speaking populations of our neighborhood, Sterling Park. Many of the English speakers moved to Sterling Park thirty years ago when it was rural, quiet, and crime-free. They raised their families, built a life, and now want to retire in peace. In the past fifteen years the town has completely changed. Though the vast majority of Spanish speakers are hard-working and honest, there have been a number of problems. The neighborhoods are clogged. Many houses have ten or more people living in them. The junior high school posts signs forbidding gang colors. There have been a number of fatal shootings in the past two years. Last summer an elderly woman was sexually assaulted four doors down from our house.

I can understand why people are mad. No one wants murder and rape in their neighborhoods. The sheriff's office holds public hearings that are marked by anger and hostility, mostly from English-speaking folks since illegal immigrants don't usually show up when the sheriff's office holds hearings. Our county supervisor even appeared on National Public Radio and said this about the urbanization and the declining quality of life in Sterling Park: "This is not urbanization. This is a cesspool. People are coming from outside of this culture and they are dumping their crap on the streets of our town. And our town is outraged that they don't get with the program."[2]

In that environment, our mostly American church has had

---

[2]Eugene Delgaudio, on *The Politics Hour: The Kojo Nnamdi Show*, June 20, 2008.

many opportunities to show love to Spanish speakers. Some of the women of the English-speaking church reached out to one Mexican woman by asking her to teach them how to make tamales (she was later deported). They spent the day together communicating through smiles and hand gestures. Later on the American women taught some of the Hispanic women how to make apple pies. People in the English-speaking church have taken offerings to buy Christmas dinner for families in the Spanish ministry and have invited Spanish speakers into their homes for Thanksgiving dinner.

My own wife is the queen of loving people from different cultures. She has absolutely no fear. She invites people who don't speak a lick of English into our house as easily as most people invite their best friends. I'll ask her ahead of time how we're going to communicate with them, in response to which she smiles and says we'll figure something out. I remember one night we had about eight men from Heriberto's work crew over to our house for dinner. They had painted the inside of the church building, and Karen wanted to say thank you. She pulled out all of the stops to honor them—Grandma's crystal and china, nice steaks, and fancy desserts. I will never forget sitting around that table and hearing, through Neissy's translation, the stories these men told of living in the refugee camps of Guatemala or picking coffee for less than a dollar a day. They spoke of the life-threatening risks they took to get into the country and of the awful pain of missing their wives and children. As they were leaving, they all thanked Karen for her hospitality, one man with tears in his eyes. He said that he had been in the country for over eight years, and this was the first time he had been inside an American's home for any reason other than to paint it.

You can see how the love of Christians adorns the gospel. The church should have a reputation in the community for extraordinary love. While nearly all of the Americans in Sterling Park direct their animosity toward Latinos, we, Guilford Baptist Church, want to gain a reputation for love and kindness that makes the Savior more attractive to them. So we have taken steps to make our love more visible to the community. When the English-speaking church outgrew the old building we were meeting in, we intentionally chose to move our meetings to a school in the heart of Sterling Park's Spanish-speaking community. Now both churches meet at the same time in the same school (down the hall from each other). All of the signs are bilingual, and we have a monthly fellowship meal together. We try everything we can to communicate the power of the gospel and so replace hate with love and reconcile enemy groups (cf. John 13:34–35; Eph. 2:18–22).

## God Is the Great Missions Director

One day a year or two ago I was having lunch with one of the original members of Guilford Fellowship. He had left after a few months of my pastorate over doctrinal issues, but there were no hard feelings. I was telling him the story of how the Spanish church was started when he stopped and laughed. "God always gets his way, doesn't he?" he said. He reminded me of how the consultant had suggested that Guilford give its building to a Spanish-speaking church, but the members were reluctant. God had, in fact, gotten his way.

So if you are a church planter or you're beginning to revitalize a church, remember that, as Tim Chester is fond of saying, "God is the great missions director." We don't need to make a ton of plans and strategies for how we are going to reach the world. God is more passionate about spreading his gospel than we are. We only need to be passionate about following his lead and trusting him for his provision. If he can use a church like ours to plant Spanish-speaking churches (we're in the process of planting a second one right now), he can use your church to do something great as well.

# 6

# How to Ruin Everything

What my people need most is my personal holiness.
**Robert Murray M'Cheyne**

I assume that the fact that you have made it this far into the book means that you are enjoying yourself. That or you lost a bet of some kind. And to this point I have enjoyed writing this book. Going back and recounting some of the ways I have seen God work has been very encouraging to my soul.

Yet I have a confession to make: I am dreading this chapter and have been for some time. But I have a sneaking suspicion that it may be the most helpful chapter in the book for some church planters.

I'll cut to the chase: planting a church can be brutal on your marriage. It almost wrecked mine. No, scratch that. My sin almost wrecked our marriage. Church planting was simply the arena in which the whole thing played out.

## Under Pressure
Look, church planting is stressful. Consider this: health researchers have put together a list of the nineteen common life changes

that cause stress.[1] Any one of those life changes by itself causes tremendous stress. But add several of them together, and you have some real significant stress. By my math, church planting almost always involves, all at once, at least half of the changes on that list.

Think about it. If you are a first-time church planter, you have a new job that is not just a new job; it's a radical change of career. And it's a job that involves a significant increase in the amount of responsibility placed on you since the whole thing rides on your decisions. You also have a new work schedule and perhaps an adverse change in your finances.

Besides the career changes, there are personal losses and adjustments as well. You have left your old church with all of your friends and support networks, which means that you may have to deal with isolation and loneliness. You have probably moved to a new town, which entails learning the ropes in a new community ("where's the Chick-fil-A?"). You will have to find a new house and move your family into it, which is about as much fun as stabbing yourself in the eye.

And the reality is that if you plant a church, those pressures will fall on your wife and family as well. They will be making all of the same adjustments that you're making. Your wife will have to deal with all of the same fears of failure that you are going through, but she won't have any control over the day-to-day operations that actually determine whether you fail. She'll have to deal with a busy and preoccupied husband.

Chances are, if your wife is like my wife, she'll want to pick up all the ministry slack that she can. Karen quickly became the church's de facto children's ministry director, women's Bible study leader, women's counselor, and janitor. I'll never forget the

---

[1]Thomas H. Holmes and M. Masusu, "Life Change and Illness Susceptibility," in *Stressful Life Events: Their Nature and Effects*, ed. Barbara S. Dohrenwend and Bruce P. Dohrenwend (New York: John Wiley & Sons), 42–72.

sight of her in the first year of our plant vacuuming the church basement on Saturday mornings while eight and a half months pregnant. Each Sunday she would ask the entire church to come over to our house for lunch so visitors would feel welcomed and the new members would get to know each other. At least twenty usually came. She wanted the church to get off the ground just as badly as I did. She is generally more gifted and fruitful than I am. And so she spent every extra ounce of her energy investing in Guilford Baptist.

The good news is that solid marriages can withstand those kinds of pressures. Good marriages even grow and thrive in such a hothouse environment as husbands and wives learn to care for each other and trust the Lord in new ways. But if you have problems in your marriage, you can be sure that the stresses of planting a church will bring the problems to the surface.

And I discovered I had some serious problems in my marriage.

## Problems

After a few months at Guilford, Karen and I began to fight. And I mean fight all the time. Constantly. We had been best friends since we were teenagers, but all of a sudden we couldn't go two days without a serious argument. I cannot remember a single thing we fought about, but we found ourselves fighting every Saturday night until the wee hours of the morning, only to go to church and then resume the conflict on Sunday night. Monday, our family day off, would usually be spent finishing the conflict or trying to recover from the damage. We were growing increasingly exhausted, angry, and hopeless.

This went on for months. It got so bad that I began to dread going to church on Sunday mornings because I was emotionally and physically worn out. I hated feeling like a hypocrite. I genuinely believed the truths that I was teaching other people, but the lessons didn't seem to be taking root in my own life and marriage. At the same time, the church was growing numerically and spiritually, and I began seeking counsel from other men about whether I should remain in the ministry. These men encouraged me to stick with the job and work the marriage out, but I knew that I couldn't hang in forever unless the marriage got better.

Then it got worse.

In the midst of our marital problems, our family went through two other significant life-events. First, we had our third child, Phineas. On the whole, Phineas's birth was a good thing; we actually like him quite a bit. But having another child can be stressful; and having three children under the age of four is especially stressful.

Second, Karen began to experience intense pain in her left eye. At first she ignored it and pushed through the pain. Now, Karen is the toughest person I have ever met. She has the pain threshold of a mixed martial arts fighter crossed with a crash-test dummy. She grew up riding her dirt bike up and down the Rocky Mountains and snowboarding on glaciers. She isn't the type to stop for anything. So we didn't think too much about the situation. Besides, we were too busy with the church.

But then her vision began to change, until she went almost completely blind in her left eye. She went to an ophthalmologist who in turn sent her to a neurologist. By this time Karen's left arm was numb and weak, and we were pretty scared. After a spinal tap and a couple of MRIs, they had a diagnosis: multiple sclerosis. The next month was filled with endless doctors' appointments, IV steroid treatments, and a lot of Internet searches.

Now, at this point you would think we would let bygones be bygones and petty marriage problems would take a backseat. But they didn't. Things continued to get worse for months and months. It's excruciating to think back on the fights that we had and some of the things that I said and did. To the outside world we looked like a model Christian husband and wife, but the reality was the opposite.

## Warning: Danger Ahead

Now, I realize this isn't a book about my marriage; it's a book about church planting. But you won't be able to plant a church if you don't get marriage right. So let me talk to you about one subtle sin inside many church planters that will tempt you to do things that are damaging to your marriage: fear of man.

Fear of man is one of the worst forms of pride. And pastoring a tiny, fledgling church will give you unending opportunities to fear men. Every Sunday you will stand in front of people, feeling like you are on trial. The committed church members will watch to see how hard you work and whether or not you are a good pastor. Strangers will also drop into your life on Sunday mornings and pass judgment. If they like you, they will stay. If they don't—and most don't—they will move on, which always tempts you to think they are taking with them your only chance to have a church that can actually pay you a salary. To make matters worse, the guys in your church planting network will watch you, checking to make sure that their church is still bigger than yours. I could keep going. All in all, your pride will tempt you to seek out the approval and applause of other people at any cost.

Even though I knew better, I cared too much about the appearance of success. I didn't just want the church to do well—I wanted it to do well in ways that were obvious to others. I wasn't willing for the building to be dirty. I wasn't willing for the children's ministry to be disorganized when visitors arrived, etc.

As a result, I took too much onto my plate and put too much onto Karen's. I never took significant time off work to take care of her when she was sick or recovering from childbirth. I left Karen at home after Phineas was born so I could lead our newly launched evening service. I didn't want the service to fail in the eyes of other people, but I didn't care about failing at home.

I also realize now that I never protected Karen from the expectations of other people in the congregation. And I never turned down her offers of help. I let her grind herself down to a nub in order to serve me and the church. I never let her know that I would love her even if she didn't kill herself to make the church go. Basically, I had no idea about how to be a good husband.

Friend, if you plant a church, please do not make the same mistake that I did. Don't believe the lie that God cannot build his church unless you neglect your wife. The God whose church you are serving is the same God who commands you to love your wife as Christ loved the church. Love your wife more than you love the opinions of other people. Prioritize her above your own success. What does it profit you to build a strong, vibrant church but forfeit your wife?

## Yet God Gives More Grace

One morning in the midst of all our marriage problems I was reading James 4, where God speaks about anger and quarreling. I felt convicted by James's piercing analysis of the self-love and self-worship that underlie our sinful conflicts. Yet after a devastating diagnosis, James gives this promise at the beginning of verse 6: "but he [God] gives more grace." I knew that's what I needed—more grace, greater grace. I needed grace that would lift us out of this mess.

Sure enough, Karen and I slowly began to see evidence of God's working in our lives. For starters, we met with some friends from Capitol Hill Baptist. As painful as this was at first, the act of bringing our lives into the light was wonderful. We no longer felt like we were keeping a secret. Now we had people to pray for us and keep us accountable.

At the same time, I was getting to know a few other pastors in the area who were part of Sovereign Grace Ministries. I noticed that they talked about their wives differently than I thought about Karen. They viewed their roles as husbands and leaders and pastors in ways that were striking—they made a real priority of caring for their wives and families. They talked about confessing sin to their wives and getting their wives' input on problems in their lives and character. I "believed" in all of these things, but these guys were actually doing it. Perhaps that was why their wives seemed to like them. And respect them! Whatever they had figured out, I wanted. Badly.

So I dragged Karen to the Sovereign Grace Pastors Conference that year. There were some great speakers—David Powlison, R. C. Sproul, C. J. Mahaney—but I wasn't interested in the talks. I just wanted the two of us to sit in the back and observe how the pastors and their wives talked to one another. Maybe we could pick up their dynamic. Somewhere in that large room, somebody had this marriage/ministry thing figured out. We just had to find them and convince them to help us.

In his kindness, the Lord brought us to just the right people. We were supposed to have lunch with the pastor and wife of the Sovereign Grace church not too far from our church, but he had to leave suddenly due to a pastoral emergency. In his place he sent their executive pastor, Vince Hinders, and Vince's wife, Bonnie. Vince and Bonnie took us to lunch and then . . . well, then Vince and Bonnie found themselves holding on for dear life as Karen and I, complete strangers, bombarded them with all of our problems. They took pity on us that afternoon and tried to help us do triage on our marriage, for which we will be forever grateful. Over the next few months they met with us several times, and though

I hardly remember everything that Vince said to me, his example and accountability were exactly what I needed.

Slowly but steadily, by God's grace, Karen and I began to forgive each other and change. A friend gave me an article from *The Journal of Biblical Counseling* titled "The Cross and Criticism," and I began to see how my inability to take criticism was holding our marriage hostage. Though I had never thought of myself as an angry person, I realized that I had let bitterness and resentment begin to dominate my life. It was an excruciating few months of learning about my sin, but in many ways it felt like Karen and I had a new lease on life.

But that's not the end of the story.

## Wait, There's More!

I had been married for almost eight years when we came to Guilford. Most of that time was peaceful and happy, even though all of the issues and problems I mentioned above were present in my life. So there were times in the midst of our marital struggles that I found myself wondering, *God, why now? If you wanted to deal with these issues in my life, why didn't you do it before I got into this church planting mess?* It seemed like a strange time for God to decide to address sin issues in my life.

But then I began to notice something. The things I was learning about my own sin—my self-deception (see Jer. 17:9), my anger, my unwillingness to take criticism—those things started showing up as points of application in my preaching. I felt like I saw those issues everywhere in Scripture.

God also gave me opportunities to use those lessons to counsel other men in the church. One day I was doing marriage counseling with a couple in our church who were good friends. Their marriage had been struggling for a long time, in large part because of the husband's short-temperedness and irritability.

When he was frustrated or in a bad mood, he would snap at his wife. So I summoned all of my counseling wisdom and told him, "Jim [not his real name], I am going to tell you something really important. This is one of the keys to being a good husband for the rest of your life. Jim, you should be nice to your wife."

Am I a great counselor or what? Be nice, I said.

The wife looked at me as if she had just realized that Mr. Rogers was her pastor. Then she said, "I think we've hit an all-time low. It's kind of depressing that you just had to tell my husband to be nice, as if we were in kindergarten."

But you know what? That sad little bit of counsel, by God's grace, took hold in Jim's life, and he began to change.

One day Jim was in my kitchen telling me about the marriage problems that some people in his family were having. He smiled at me and said, "You know, I had *the talk* with the husband." I asked him what he meant. He said, "You know, the talk . . . the 'you should be nice to your wife' talk. I think it helped him." We both laughed, but it hit me. God sent Vince Hinders to have the talk with me, so that I could have the talk with my friend Jim, so that Jim could then have the talk with someone else.

That's how this works. God is in the business of making us holy and effective, even if it's painful.

So if you plant a church, be prepared for the fact that God may begin to sharpen and sanctify you in ways that are difficult. But take heart in the fact that God will use it. Just as Paul comforted others with the comfort he received from God (2 Cor. 1:4), we too help others grow in holiness when God puts us through a season of sanctification.

# 7

# No Offense, but You're Doing Everything Wrong

I was sitting at lunch with Bob Donohue, a friend of mine who pastors in a next-door suburb. We had been talking about the growth of Guilford Baptist, together with the fact that the growth was killing me, when he pulled out the old "iron fist in a velvet glove" routine. You know, soften a piece of biting criticism with encouragement. Bob affirmed, "Mike, I think you are doing a great job. God is doing a lot of things through you at Guilford." *Great, thanks, Bob. Now what do you really want to say?* He continued, "But with all due respect, I have to say that I think you are doing everything totally wrong."

*Everything totally wrong? Don't hold back on me now, Bob.*

The church had grown steadily over the course of its first year and a half. There were over a hundred and thirty English-speaking people in the church, and I was stressed-out. Karen and I were spending a great deal of our time helping new people assimilate into the congregation. Almost everyone who joined the church had been into our home for a meal. And we enjoyed this. Karen is a master of hospitality and was using her gifts to build the church.

But it had become too much. People were in our home at least two or three times a week. We began a line item in our family budget just to accommodate all the food Karen purchased for hospitality. Yet we realized that relatively few other people in the church were connecting and serving each other. Everyone in the church was connecting to our family, but there was relatively little ministry and community happening apart from us. The situation was becoming both tiring and unmanageable. We were near the saturation point.

When I was finished describing the situation to Bob, he offered his assessment: I had done everything backward. Instead of spending all my time making sure that new people were assimilated into the church, I should have spent more of my time training new leaders in the church. He compared the growth of the church to the growth of the human body: the muscles and organs of the church were growing, but I hadn't done anything to build a solid skeleton. As a result, we found ourselves growing into a blob with no infrastructure. Even though we had just installed two new elders, one of them was investing all of his time working with the Spanish church. We didn't have enough leadership for the people we had, let alone enough leadership to accommodate the new people who came week to week.

## Interlude: Get to Know Other Pastors

Can I pause here just to plug the value of friendships with pastors at other churches, especially when you're flying solo? Few things have been as worthwhile as the time that I have spent getting to know the other pastors in our area. My goal has been to meet one pastor every month. I email them, tell them who I am, let them know that our church has been praying for them (it's our practice to pray for other churches every Sunday morning), and ask if I can buy them lunch. They usually pay since they are older and more established, but it seems rude not to offer up front. At lunch, I ask them tons of questions about their ministry, their families, and their knowledge of the community.

For the most part, you would be amazed at how much other pastors know and what good advice they have, even the guys who are (shudder) not theologically Reformed. Not every guy is incredibly discerning, but you can learn something from just about anyone. Almost every good ministry idea I've ever had has been "borrowed" from another pastor.

So if you're a church planter or a young pastor, get to know the other pastors in your area. If you're an older pastor, get to know the new guys in town and help them out a little.

## Qualities of a Leader

Now back to the story line. Sitting at lunch with Bob, I was hit by the wisdom of his diagnosis as well as by the necessary prescription. I needed to develop more leaders, more people who could carry on the work of the ministry.

God calls men to be leaders in the church and at home, and so the natural place to first focus my attention was on the men of the congregation. I envisioned a group of men upon whom I could depend to help move the church in the right direction.

I started by outlining the profile of what a man in our church should look like. I listed five qualities:

1) *He should be godly.* If a man is going to help take the church forward, he needs to be growing in holiness. He should be regular in his practice of the spiritual disciplines, blameless in his behavior (avoiding blatant sins like pornography, drunkenness, and cheating), and increasingly putting to death the

more subtle sins in his life like pride, anger, and selfishness. He should evidence the fruit of God's Spirit and a growing trust in God's providence.

2) *He should be theologically solid.* The church needs men who have a firm grasp on theological matters. A man who is a good leader should be able to understand the doctrines that are at the heart of our congregation. He needs to be able to comprehend and explain to others what we believe about the Trinity, the doctrine of Scripture, election, and so on.

3) *He should do a good job leading his family.* If a man's not leading his home well, he can't ultimately be a useful and effective leader in the church. He should be leading his wife to grow in godliness, loving her sacrificially, and taking care of her emotionally. He should be discipling his kids and teaching them to love the gospel.

4) *He should be involved in the church.* Even if a guy is holy and theologically solid, he's not much use to the church unless he understands the importance of the church and is committed to seeing it grow and prosper. A man should lead his family to serve in the church. He should be involved in greeting visitors on Sunday mornings, discipling younger believers, and sharing the gospel with his friends and neighbors.

5) *He should understand what makes Christian leadership distinctive.* He should not lord his authority over other people but should be the chief servant (Mark 10:42–45). His leadership should be gracious and patient. He should understand the principles of biblical life change and know how to bring them to bear on the lives of others.

When I looked at the five qualities I had written out, I realized that I had basically summarized the biblical qualifications for an elder, with the exception of the requirement that an elder be able to teach. I began to dream about the idea of raising up a host of men like this to act as the skeleton for the church.

## Training Men

The only question was how to get those qualities off the piece of paper and into the lives of the men in our church. I was already feeling overwhelmed by my schedule, and I was still learning all of these things myself. Where to begin?

Fortunately I had friends, including Bob, that iron-fist-in-velvet buddy of mine. Bob sent me a giant three-ring binder with the materials that he used in his church's leadership training program.[1] Using reading assignments from Wayne Grudem's *Bible Doctrine* (coauthored with Jeff Purswell) and other materials, the program covered most of the major topics in systematic theology as well as sanctification, leadership, and evangelism. Nothing in a church's life can accomplish what the weekly preaching of the Word to the whole church accomplishes. Yet these lessons, stretched out over twenty-two meetings, would give me the chance to target temporarily an area of acute need. It would give me an opportunity to build these five qualities in our men. Now I had a plan.

So I put the word out to the guys in the church. At first I wasn't sure whether I should choose a small group who showed the most potential for leadership or open it up to anyone who would commit to attending. I decided on the latter since I figured that the more men I could pour into at once, the better. I announced that we would meet for two hours on every third Saturday morning. It was a weird schedule, but guys with young families (myself included) probably should not commit to being out of the house every other Saturday morning.

I figured the time commitment, the long assigned read-

---

[1]See Appendix 2 for the syllabus.

ings, and the required Scripture memorization would keep the turnout low. But I was wrong—we had fifteen guys at our first meeting. I talked about the group. I told them that the homework wasn't optional, that the Scripture memorization would be recited in front of the group, that attendance was mandatory, and that everyone had to commit to being open about their lives. Surely these requirements would drive away at least half the group. Wrong again—at the next meeting we had seventeen guys.

In that first meeting, we considered the first three chapters of Ephesians and saw that what was at stake in the local church was nothing less than a display of God's glory to the universe. We saw that male leadership in the church and home was crucial to whether or not Guilford Baptist would grow and prosper. And I spoke frankly about the needs of the church and the fact that I had stretched myself beyond my capacity to try and meet those needs alone.

The response was good. I'm not going to lie to you and say that revival broke out or that all of the men grew into super-leaders overnight. But we did notice a steady, consistent growth in the lives of most of the guys. As we studied theology, we always wrestled with the question, How does this apply to me as I try to be a faithful leader in my home and church?

Through it all, a group of guys who could be relied upon were growing up. They had wrestled with the doctrine of election; they could explain why the inspiration of Scripture leads to its authority; and they knew why it matters that Jesus' death on the cross was a substitutionary sacrifice and not merely a moral example.

As time went on, we moved out of systematic theology into matters of sanctification. Some of our conversations were so fruitful that we had to suspend our normal schedule and extend them over subsequent meetings. Our discussion about pride was an eye-opener as guys began to see the negative fruit of their pride throughout their lives. Our discussion about anger lasted three meetings as guys considered how their outbursts of anger, small and large, pointed to a deeper problem with their worship. We talked frankly about lust, pornography, and sinful behaviors issuing from those patterns of sin. We spent one meeting talking about the blessings of sex and romance within marriage. Guys started to step up and do a better job of leading their families and being involved in the congregation. When it came time in the church to identify small-group leaders and new elders, we were able to choose from this pool of trained men.

## Real Men, Real Leaders

Now, there's a lot of talk these days in church circles about manliness. It's popular to decry the "sissification" of the church. According to an article in *Christianity Today*, one pastor, for instance, "argues that 'latte-sipping Cabriolet drivers' do not represent biblical masculinity, because 'real men'—like Jesus, Paul, and John the Baptist— are 'dudes: heterosexual, win-a-fight, punch-you-in-the-nose dudes.' In other words, because Jesus is not a 'limp-wristed, dress-wearing hippie,' the men created in his image are not sissified church boys; they are aggressive, assertive, and nonverbal."[2]

I am not completely unsympathetic to the point. I think NCAA and NFL football is compelling evidence that there is a Creator who loves us. Somewhere deep in my heart I have a conviction that men should change the oil in their cars. I love tattoos and own a reciprocating saw. I get the whole "be a tough guy" thing. Yet we all know that being a real man has nothing to do with any of that. It doesn't have anything to do with your clothes, the car that you drive (for the record, I rock a tricked-out 1998

---

[2]Brandon O'Brien, "A Jesus for Real Men," *Christianity Today*, Vol. 52, No. 4 (April 18, 2008).

Mercury Tracer station wagon), your favorite beverage, or the size of your biceps (again, for the record, mine are about twenty-eight inches each, but that's just a rough guess).

Instead, being a real man means being responsible, dependable, humble, and strong. It means pouring yourself out for your wife and kids. It means walking closely with Christ and taking care of people in need. Seriously, who cares what kind of clothes a guy wears? Who cares what kind of car he drives? What could possibly be more irrelevant? I have guys in my church who are loud, big, and dedicated to mixed martial arts and beer. And I have guys who are soft-spoken, cerebral, and oblivious to sports and cars. Guess who are more of a headache for me as a pastor? And guess who are more reliable, faithful, dependable, and better husbands and fathers? I'm not convinced that the way to raise up men in my church is to run around like some pro-Jesus hybrid of Tim "The Toolman" Taylor and Steve McQueen. Instead, men need to be taught, trained, and challenged and then set loose to serve God with their individual personalities and temperaments.

Churches should be careful not to judge leaders by the standards of the world. The world may be captivated by power, charisma, machismo, prestige, physical beauty, wealth, and strength, but these are not the qualities that draw the attention of the New Testament authors. Consider Paul's instructions to Titus:

> Appoint elders in every town as I directed you—if anyone is above reproach, the husband of one wife, and his children are believers and not open to the charge of debauchery or insubordination. For an overseer, as God's steward, must be above reproach. He must not be arrogant or quick-tempered or a drunkard or violent or greedy for gain, but hospitable, a lover of good, self-controlled, upright, holy, and disciplined.

He must hold firm to the trustworthy word as taught, so that
he may be able to give instruction in sound doctrine and also
to rebuke those who contradict it. (Titus 1:5b–9)

By and large, the world will not applaud a man for being hos-
pitable and self-controlled. And too often, neither do churches.

After I became a Christian I grew up in a nondenominational
mega-church. To my knowledge, almost every one of the church's
thirty-plus elders were successful professionals (lawyers, doctors, captains of industry). Some of them were godly shepherds,
but a number of them, by their own admission, were not very
knowledgeable about the Bible and were not interested in caring for individual members. They had the qualities necessary to
lead in the workplace, so the church assumed they could lead the
congregation. But they should not have assumed this. This is a
real danger for the church.

Churches should, on the other hand, expect that the Lord
has given gifts of leadership to men from different ethnicities,
different levels of education, and different socioeconomic backgrounds. In fact, given Scripture's teaching on God's preference
for using the poor and lowly to do his will (cf. 1 Sam. 16:7; Luke
1:46–49; 1 Cor. 1:26–29), we should expect that many church
leaders will be unimpressive in the eyes of the world. If all of our
leaders look like they belong in the boardroom of a Fortune 500
company, we're probably doing something wrong.

One time I had the ear of Steve Timmis, a church planter
and author in the UK. I began to talk to him about the lack of
leadership that I saw in our church, and he challenged me at
this point. He observed that the apostle Paul planted churches
and established elders within a relatively short period of time.
For example, Paul planted the church in Ephesus (Acts 19). He
ministered there from the late summer of A.D. 52 to the spring

or early summer of A.D. 55.[3] When a riot broke out, he moved on to Macedonia. After some time sailing around, Paul landed at Miletus, and we read in Acts 20 that he called the elders of the church at Ephesus to himself. In other words, Paul was able to plant the Ephesian church and raise up elders in those first three years. How theologically sophisticated or professionally accomplished could these men have been?

The ascended Christ kindly promises to provide leaders for his church (Eph. 4:7–12). If there is a dearth of leadership in our congregation, it may be that we are looking for the wrong things or that we haven't done the work of developing the right things.

## Conclusion

Friend, if you are going to plant or revitalize a church, know in advance that even moderate church growth will become a burden if you haven't developed the people who can help with the ministry. Don't invest all your efforts in bringing in more people before you have done the hard work of cultivating leaders.

Good leaders, both those who hold recognized offices and those in the wider congregation, are gifts from God that you should seek and develop.

---

[3]F. F. Bruce, *New Testament History* (New York: Doubleday, 1980), 326.

# 8

# Redefine
# *Extraordinary*

As I stand on the brink of my fourth anniversary as the pastor at Guilford, I realize that the end of this story is not even close to being written. In all honesty, it's a little embarrassing to write this book so early on in my pastoral career. It's a little like getting a tattoo when you are eighteen years old; it clearly expresses what you were thinking and feeling at the time, but you will probably live to regret making a permanent record. I have some pretty goofy tattoos that remind me of this truth each morning as I look in the mirror ("Barry Manilow 4-Eva" . . . what was I thinking?).

But allow me a few pages here at the conclusion to make several observations and talk a bit about my plans for the future . . . and hopefully yours.

## What Young Men Tend to Underestimate

I hope to be buried at Guilford Baptist. Not literally, of course, since there are probably county health regulations that would prevent this. And I hope not anytime soon. Yet I do intend to stay here for the rest of my life. I want to conduct the funeral of every person in that church until it's my turn in the box. (Note to Karen: when it's my time, pose my body in a creek somewhere like a crime scene from *Law & Order* . . . you only get one body, so let's enjoy it!). That's my plan. Of course, we never know the Lord's appointed plan for our lives (see Acts 18:21; James 4:13–16), so I might not be here next month. But intentions are important, even if we cannot control whether or not they are fulfilled.

As a general rule, I think pastors should stay where they are and tend the flock long-term. Mark Dever has observed that a fruitful pastor must "preach and pray, love and stay." If we are doing our jobs well, then our sermons, our prayers, and our love will be exponentially more effective the longer we stay in one place. As one old man at Capitol Hill Baptist Church always used to say, "Young men tend to overestimate what they can accomplish in the short term and underestimate what they can accomplish in the long term."

Many pastors appear to use their church to move up the professional ladder, going from small to medium to large churches that pay them well in money and prestige. Our goal as pastors should be instead to plant ourselves in the lives of our people, to put down deep roots in the community, and to grow in the pot in which we're planted. If you are finding it difficult to be faithful, joyful, and fruitful in your current context, it's doubtful that a change of scenery will cure that.

I know there are exceptions to this rule. Bad situations and wonderful opportunities both can make moving on a wise choice. But we must remember that pride and love of money are powerful motivators.

## Obsessing over Church Size

So this is it. This is the point in the book where I'm supposed to impress you. I'm supposed to pull back the curtain and show you a gigantic church and then explain, "This could all be yours if you go and do likewise." Of course, none of that would be true. Guilford Baptist is a very ordinary church.

We normally have around two hundred adults and older kids attend on Sunday mornings. That would be huge in the Highlands of Scotland perhaps, but not in the United States. During the summer, when people are on vacation and the college kids are back home, we have fewer. During the school year and during special events, we have more.

It could be that by the time this book is published, we'll have four hundred. And it could be that half the church will have been relocated by their companies or deported by the INS. But you do realize, don't you, that numbers don't ultimately matter?

Let me be straightforward. The obsession with church size is *killing* many church planters. I used to drop in occasionally on a gathering of local church planters. There was a running tension in the group—everyone either subtly bragged about the size of his church (while trying to seem like they weren't) or made excuses for it.

Many guys who serve faithfully, pastor well, preach clearly, and love their flocks will not see overwhelming and immediate fruit from their efforts. Oftentimes those men become discouraged because they believe that in order to be a good pastor, you have to have a large congregation.

I had lunch with a friend the other day. He took over as the pastor of a very small church about a year ago and is working to reform it. He is preaching God's Word, evangelizing the lost, discipling believers, straightening out issues with church government. He is doing a good job. But the church hasn't "taken off." It's grown some, but not a ton. It's still a little wobbly in places. There's nothing particularly impressive about the church to the rest of the world. He confessed over lunch that he struggles with discouragement. Things both inside him (his pride) and outside him (all the books on church planting and church growth) encouraged him to equate "big church" with "good pastor" and "small church" with "second-rate pastor." I have heard this story over and over.

You may have heard it as well. Have you ever read the blog of a church planter? Invariably you get one of two stories. Either you get reports of wild success ("We saw 73,239 accept Jesus in our forty services this week. And the music guys brought down the house!") or you will read a report that, while it's not an outright lie, is definitely a sanitized and airbrushed version of the truth.

You will almost never read anyone speak honestly about their struggles. You won't read an honest report about the Sunday when barely anyone showed up. You won't read about a church planter's frustrations with a lack of visible fruit. And if you do read any of these things, you can be pretty sure that he's paving the way for announcing in the not too distant future that he's moving to another church.

Why is that so? I think it's because we have wrongly put pressure on ordinary pastors to do the extraordinary. Through books, television, the Internet, and the ever-growing culture of celebrity in evangelicalism, we have essentially defined *successful pastor* as one who pastors a giant church. As a result, many church planters are tempted to water down the gospel in order to draw a crowd (and let's face it, it is not too hard to draw a crowd; brothels and methadone clinics are packed full on most days). Meanwhile, the pastors who don't want to build their churches on something other than a robust gospel are left feeling like failures if the church doesn't grow quickly.

Don't misunderstand me. This is not a "small is beautiful" rant against big churches. Having grown up in a large church, I do happen to prefer smaller ones. I'd rather pastor a church that stays relatively small but plants ten other churches. That's my personal preference. But I'm not going to say that all large churches are sellouts and that small-church pastors are the only ones keeping it real. To be sure, there are truly wretched small churches, and there are truly wonderful large churches. God has gifted and placed some men so that their influence and ministry will reach many, many people. As long as they are faithful to the gospel, we should be exceedingly glad for their ministries and praise God for the fruit he bears through them.

But I hope you realize that is not God's call for most of our ministries. Most pastors in the world will never pastor a church of much more than a couple hundred people.

A few weeks ago I called an older pastor in the area whom I hadn't met before. We run in the same theological circles, so it was strange that we hadn't met. I suggested that we grab lunch sometime, and he kindly obliged. As we sat down, he apologized for not getting in touch with me earlier. He explained, though, that he had grown weary of meeting young pastors as they moved into the community to plant churches. He said, "I take them out to lunch and listen to them go on and on about how they are here to reach the whole county with the gospel. They all talk about how big their church is going to be and how they are going to be the next _____. Fill in the name of your favorite superstar pastor. I sit there restraining the urge to yell at them, 'No, you're not! If you are exceedingly hard-working and blessed by God, you will plant a healthy church that serves God faithfully! I have spent five minutes with you, and I can tell that you're not *that* talented!'"

He was being a little facetious, of course, but his point is borne out by his experience. Most church planters will never pastor huge churches. Are all these men failures? Are they second-rate servants of God? If not, why do so many pastors and church planters *feel* like failures?

## Redefine *Extraordinary*

Here's my solution, and in many ways the main point I want to make with this book: I want to redefine *extraordinary*. I don't think that it's wrong for church planters and church revitalizers to long for an extraordinary ministry. After all, we serve an extraordinary God who has procured an extraordinary salvation by extraordinary means. We should expect extraordinary things to happen when we serve him. Yet we need to come to grips with the fact that the extraordinary things that God does may not be immediately and outwardly extraordinary in the eyes of other people.

What should we count as God's extraordinary work? It's not a stadium-sized building, a multi-million dollar budget, or satellite feeds to multiple venues. That's how the world measures and achieves *extraordinary*. Rather, it's extraordinary when God converts our neighbors, coworkers, children, friends, and family. It's extraordinary when proud, angry, selfish people have their hearts changed by the gospel. It's extraordinary when new churches selflessly invest their time, money, and prayers to establish and multiply even newer congregations. It's extraordinary when marriages are restored and cultural prejudices give way to unity in the gospel of Christ. It's extraordinary whenever God uses "normal" pastors and church planters, faithful men with ordinary gifts and talents, to do all this work.

In Romans, Paul writes that "from Jerusalem and all the way around to Illyricum I have fulfilled the ministry of the gospel of Christ" (15:19). Leon Morris observes in his commentary on Romans that Paul made this statement even though he had only planted several churches in the larger cities of the region. How then could Paul consider the ministry "fulfilled"? What about the rest of the area? Morris concludes that Paul must have expected that the new churches he had planted in the major cities would take the gospel to the far-flung regions.[1]

The local church is God's plan to extend his gospel of grace to the whole world. He scatters unimpressive clusters of believers everywhere to extend his saving reign. The local church proclaims the gospel, lives out the gospel, and gives evidence to the truth of the gospel by its love and service to those inside and outside the congregation. When you plant a church, you are signing on to God's plan for God's purposes. It's up to you to be faithful as you depend on God's grace to carry out your appointed task. God will use your labors to do his will. It could be that your congregation is meant to be a larger piece of the overall picture, or it could be that it's meant to be a smaller piece. Either way, don't forget the privilege it is to be even a "small" part of God's marvelous plan. It's an extraordinary calling.

## Extraordinary People, Extraordinary Promises

Many church planters and revitalizers suffer from a perspective problem. We preach a spiritual message, but functionally we live like materialists. We look around at the things that we can touch, feel, measure, and count, and we calibrate our sense of success on those things alone.

But it shouldn't be so. The Bible makes amazing statements about the church, and these statements aren't qualified in any way by church size or age.

The author of Hebrews tells us what happens when a local congregation gathers together to worship God. It gives us a glimpse of our one heavenly and eschatological assembly!

[1]Leon Morris, *The Epistle to the Romans* (Grand Rapids: Eerdmans, 1998), 514. I heard Dr. Morris's point also made by Dave Harvey at the 2009 Sovereign Grace Pastors Conference. It is also referenced in Steve Timmis and Tim Chester, *Total Church* (Nottingham, UK: Inter-Varsity Press, 2007), 102. This book is also available from Crossway Books. I am not sure through which source I first became aware of it, so I'll credit all of them.

> But you have come to Mount Zion and the city of the living
> God, the heavenly Jerusalem, and to the innumerable angels
> in festal gathering, and to the assembly of the firstborn who
> are enrolled in heaven, and to God, the judge of all, and to
> the spirits of the righteous made perfect, and to Jesus, the
> mediator of a new covenant, and to the sprinkled blood that
> speaks a better word than the blood of Abel. . . . Therefore
> let us be grateful for receiving a kingdom that cannot be
> shaken, and thus let us offer to God acceptable worship,
> with reverence and awe, for our God is a consuming fire.
> (12:22–24, 28–29)

Did you catch that? When a church engages in corporate
worship, it enters into spiritual communion with innumerable
angels and the spirits of the righteous in heaven. When we come
to worship together, we come to the Lord Jesus Christ himself.
Friend, that is the definition of *extraordinary*! Who really cares
how many people are standing in the room with you at that time?
Who cares how unimpressive and ordinary your gathering is to
the eyes of the world? Your congregation's reverent and awe-
filled praises come before the living God, who is a consuming
fire! Besides, if you count all of the angels and believers in heaven
that join their praises to yours, your attendance numbers actually exceed those of the mega-church down the street, humanly
speaking!

Finally, look at the promises that God's Word holds out to
those who serve the church faithfully as pastors. The apostle
Peter writes to the elders of the embattled church:

> So I exhort the elders among you, as a fellow elder and a
> witness of the sufferings of Christ, as well as a partaker in
> the glory that is going to be revealed, shepherd the flock
> of God that is among you, exercising oversight, not under
> compulsion, but willingly, as God would have you; not for
> shameful gain, but eagerly; not domineering over those in

your charge, but being examples to the flock. And when the Chief Shepherd appears, you will receive the unfading crown of glory. (1 Pet. 5:1–4)

An "unfading crown of glory." That's an extraordinary promise. There is nothing in this passage about the size of your church. There is nothing about how famous you become as a pastor. No; elders and shepherds and overseers and pastors are simply told to be faithful. We are commanded to be "eager" and "willing" and gentle to the flock of God. If we are, we will receive "the unfading crown of glory." I can't begin to imagine what that means, but I am sure it is really, really good.

So, friend, if you are so called by the Lord, I hope you revitalize a dead church or start a new one. If you are already neck-deep in the work, then I hope that you renew and redouble your commitment to the task at hand.

Or if you are an established pastor or church leader, I hope you begin to think about how you can plant new churches or revitalize old ones in your area and around the world. But if you do, do it for the reasons we have considered. Do it because of the amazing ways that God uses ordinary, faithful churches for his glory.

I'll see you when the Chief Shepherd gets here.

# appendix 1

# Church Planting Memo Prepared by Mark Dever for the Elders at CHBC

Memo on Church Planting (Sept. 2004)

From: Mark Dever

To: The Elders

On Tuesday (Sept. 7) & Wednesday (Sept. 8) Mike McKinley & I drove to Philadelphia for a couple of days talking and praying about church planting, his role, pastoral ministry, CHBC, etc. On the way up, Mike rehearsed again for me his testimony, giving a longer version, and his maturing in ministry conviction and sense of calling. He expressed great thanks to God, and to CHBC for what he and Karen have already experienced here.

He told me that he is currently discipling four men. Karen has taken initiative with a number of women, and is thinking how she can reach out to non-Christian ladies in evangelism.

We read carefully through the church statement of faith and the church covenant, and Mike had no disagreements or hesitancies about affirming them. We spent about an hour reading through the constitution and discussing it. He affirmed the evident wisdom of the way things had been set out.

We then looked at Mike's map of the area, designating who and where those members are who live in the area, but outside of the District, Arlington and Alexandria. We spent quite a bit of time going through the membership directory and considering people who could be especially helpful in a church plant. We came up with a list of 103 people that I suggested he concentrate on. They include some in the core area, but more in southeastern Maryland or out west in Virginia (anywhere from Burke to Sterling). The parts of Maryland north of the District seem to have too few of our members to be a viable place, and therefore of less use to us. I've asked Mike to keep me updated on who he is talking to about being involved in the church plant. And we've talked about the possibility of Mike & Karen leading two different community groups, with the groups' memberships composed from these 103 church members (perhaps with each meeting once a month on Friday night, then they could have a meeting every other week). We also spent more than an hour going over outside-of-CHBC people he could contact.

The second day we discussed various ways that CHBC could do a church plant with Mike as the pastor. There are a number of variables to consider, among them:

*1a. whether Mike would be an elder at CHBC before he goes,*

*1b. and whether any other elders would go with him*

*1c. and whether we would send Mike out with two other elders or not*

*2. whether it would be left to CHBC or to the new congregation to recognize their first set of elders (that is, would the congregation of CHBC or only those members going to constitute the new church elect the first two elders to accompany Mike)*

*3. where the church plant is (where our interested members are, distance from CHBC, either church we would inhabit or lack of good churches in an area, general population growth, an area populated by internationals)*

*4. if it's going to an already established church or starting a new one,*

*5a. if any CHBC members would go and if so*

*5b. how many*

*5c. and who,*

*5d. and why they would go (we ask them, they respond to general call, their relationship with Mike and Karen, they live near where the church plant would be)*

*6a. when this would happen*

*6b. and how long the public preparation would be,*

*6c. what would be the stages of public preparation*

*7a. what kind of financial support would be given*

*7b. and for how long.*

*8a. whether Mike would be affiliated/supported by another group*

*8b. SBCV?*

*8c. NAMB?*

*9. What we would expect of the new church*

*9a. Same statement of faith*

*9b. Same church covenant*

*9c. Congregational with plural eldership*

*9d. Baptistic*

*9e. reformed*

*9f. expositional preaching central*

*9g. cooperate with 9Marks ministries*

*9h. nothing else [e.g., music style, casual dress, small group structure, evangelism practices, denominational affiliation]*

Let's think now about each of these considerations, in turn:

*1a. whether Mike would be an elder at CHBC before he goes.* It is my opinion that he should, and should be so recognized as soon as possible. If we don't think he's qualified to be an elder, he shouldn't be being supported by us as a potential church planter. Certainly his ministry among our congregation will be more slight by the time of any appointment (within the year) to the eldership than would any other previously recognized elder (save myself and Michael Lawrence), but that seems to be part of what it means to call a church planter from outside our congregation. Mike and Karen have begun ministering among us, and I have no doubt will continue to be a blessing among a broader portion of our membership than simply those who would go with them. At this point, Mike is focused on church planting, but is also committed to the wider pastoral care of the CHBC congregation. I think Mike is biblically qualified to be an elder, and should be so nominated and recognized as early as possible so as to best prepare our congregation and himself for the church plant.

*1b. and whether any other elders would go with him.* Not

necessarily, but ideally. It would be best to have (as the CHBC constitution requires) two unpaid elders to assist Mike. Whether they would be currently serving elders at CHBC or simply CHBC members whom Mike is confident his new congregation could and would recognize as elders is another question.

*ic. and whether we would send Mike out with two other elders or not.* This would be ideal, but not necessary.

*2. whether it would be left to CHBC or to the new congregation to recognize their first set of elders (that is, would the congregation of CHBC or only those members going to constitute the new church elect the first two elders to accompany Mike).* Even if CHBC elders are sent with Mike and initially serve in this capacity, as soon as McKinley Memorial Baptist Tabernacle is constituted (or whatever he would chose to name it) that congregation would need to affirm or deny the currently serving elders. It is possible that CHBC members who would go with Mike could be recognized as elders by his church plant that CHBC would in prudence not recognize as elders in our congregation at this time.

*3. where the church plant is (where our interested members are, distance from CHBC, either church we would inhabit or lack of good churches in an area, general population growth, an area populated by internationals).* Our interested members are most likely in one of three places—either in the core area and would move out to where the church plant would be, already living in Southern Maryland (from Bladensburg south) or living west of here in Virginia from Burke to Herndon. It is preferable that the new church plant be further from CHBC both to better serve the members who already live in that area, and to help make the church plant more viable. An existing congregation in the District, Arlington or Alexandria we may decide is providentially identified to us. Mike will be spending part of his time researching the church situation in the two areas just identified. God has already providentially given CHBC many contacts with other local churches, and we trust these will be used to good advantage in our efforts to church plant.

*4. if it's going to an already established church or starting a new one.* There are advantages both ways, but we would prefer taking a poor or ailing church and refurbishing its witness to the gospel in the community. Failing this, we would certainly act to begin a new congregation.

**5a. if any CHBC members would go and if so.** It is possible that Mike could go out from us with no members accompanying him and the church turn-around or plant still succeed. God gives life through the preaching of His Word, and we know that Mike is committed to this. Our preference would be that some number of members go with him, both to help establish the work, and to make space here for new members.

**5b. how many.** This seems to depend almost entirely on the answer to 5d, why they would go. We hope that the number will be large enough to encourage Mike and Karen in the work, and to make their support viable, but not so large as to disrupt the work at CHBC. We would imagine from a handful to fifty, but if 100 want to go, we would trust God's providence! A lot depends on who the individuals are.

**5c. and who.** This, again, would largely depend on the answer to 5d. Obviously people must themselves choose to go and be a part of this. Part of their willingness to go could be respect for CHBC's vision in this, but part of it must also be their recognition of Mike's ministry, their desire to support him in this, their desire to see a congregation established in the place selected, and probably their ability to live near the church plant and perhaps their relationships with others who commit to be involved in the new congregation. If the C's go because the B's go (or at least as part of the reason) that should be recognized as natural and good.

**5d. and why they would go (we ask them, they respond to general call, their relationship with Mike and Karen, they live near where the church plant would be).** We can imagine a number of reasons they should go. Ideally, it would *not* be because of a deep dissatisfaction with CHBC (perhaps other than with its size). People may go because we ask them specifically for their help. They themselves might simply feel moved by what they hear being announced publicly, as vision is created for a church in a particular community. Some may want to go because of relationships that God develops between them and Mike and Karen. Some may want

to get involved because they live in or near the community of the
new church plant.

**6a. when this would happen.** We can't know. But we would
like to see this congregation established by July 1, 2006. Obviously
we can't know this, but it seems like a good date to shoot for. If we
end up partnering with an established congregation, it could be
much sooner. It is probably best that Mike not leave CHBC earlier
than July 1, 2005, however, for the sake of his own training and
relationships. We understand his time to be at CHBC kind of like a
medical residency, getting him ready by experience for practicing
on his own.

**6b. and how long the public preparation would be.** Again this
depends on the variables, but ideally about a year, where the congregation can know, have input, pray and individuals can decide
what their participation will be. This could be altered if we end up
partnering with an existing church that is desperate.

**6c. what would be the stages of public preparation.** Deciding
and announcing where the plant/recovery would be, and then
giving people sufficient time to sort out who would go as part of
this. We would encourage the group (self-identified, but with the
blessing of the elders) to meet separately with Mike for prayer and
planning. How many, regularly and for how long these meetings
would be held will be determined by other factors.

**7a. what kind of financial support would be given.** This will
depend on what is needed. An existing congregation that we partner with may be financially viable itself. Even apart from that, the
number of members going may make at least paying Mike's salary and hiring a meeting place possible without CHBC's financial
help. This would have to be sorted out with the understanding that
CHBC is committed to the viability of the new congregation, but
that the new congregation must show itself committed as well.

**7b. and for how long.** NAMB/SBCV funding for church planters
is, I think 3 years (full support 1st year; diminishing sharply each
of the two years after). I would suggest that we pledge Mike full
financial support for the first year (even if the new congregation
could afford paying him before that). Financial support beyond
the first year would depend upon what we see happening in the

new congregation. Given Mike's own gifts, the people who go with him, and the existing congregation (if we partner), we would hope that the new congregation would be able to pay Mike's salary fully beginning one year after they constitute. If they couldn't we (CHBC elders) would need to evaluate either the place we've selected, the quality of Mike's work or the members from our congregation that have gone in order to decide our course of action.

*8. whether Mike would be affiliated/supported by another group.*

*8a. SBCV?* Mike will look into this and give us recommendations.

*8b. NAMB?* Mike will look into this and give us recommendations.

*9. What we would expect of the new church.*

*9a. Same statement of faith.* It's a good statement. Or the existing church's statement, depending upon what it is (would need CHBC elders' approval).

*9b. Same church covenant.* Or something similar.

*9c. Congregational with plural eldership.* We're not planning a Sovereign Grace church, nor do we want Mike to have to serve without fellow elders. At the same time, if he goes to an existing congregation without elders, there may need to be some flexibility in moving to a plurality of elders. This should be understood and accepted by the congregation up front.

*9d. Baptistic.* This is non-negotiable. We don't care if it's in the name. Though I think it's more honorable to have it in the name, but it's not essential. That the congregation would require believer baptism for membership is, however, necessary for us to support the work.

*9e. reformed.* Like CHBC is.

*9f. expositional preaching central.* This is foundational to a healthy church. Mike is committed to this. That's not saying that his sermons need to be an hour long!

*9g. cooperate with 9Marks ministries.* If for any reason Mike didn't want to, we would want to know why. He should work to have a healthy church himself, and get his congregation to work to spread that among other pastors and church leaders.

*9h. nothing else [e.g., music style, casual dress, small group structure, evangelism practices, denominational affiliation].* Many things are matters of prudence and the personality of the pastor, elders, membership, location, etc. All these other matters must be left to the discretion of the leaders and ultimately the membership of the other congregation.

**In conclusion:**

Mike will be working on developing relationships, scouting out churches in the two designated areas, following up on other leads, and getting us a recommendation on pursuing either SBCV or NAMB funding. This recommendation he will have to the elders by December 1, 2004. Mike will be giving me weekly reports at staff meeting on progress on establishing relationships with people in the congregation, and particularly (though not only) with those interested in church planting. At the elders' discretion, Mike will happily give updates on his work to the elders, at a members' meeting or in a Sunday evening service for prayer. Even apart from elder action on this, I will probably ask Mike to share sometimes in the Sunday evening service depending on some specific matter the congregation should know and pray about.

# appenDIX 2
# Men's Discipleship Training Syllabus: Grace Community Church (Ashburn, Virginia)

## Introduction
### 1. Systematic Theology
Chapter 1 from *Bible Doctrine* by Wayne Grudem
Explanation of group goals
Scripture Memory—1 Timothy 4:6

## The Doctrine of Scripture
### 2. Authority, Inerrancy, Clarity, Necessity and Sufficiency of the Bible
Chapters 2 & 3 from *Bible Doctrine*
Scripture Memory—II Timothy 3:16

## The Doctrine of God
### 3. Communicable and Incommunicable Attributes
Chapters 4 & 5 from *Bible Doctrine*
Scripture Memory—Exodus 34:6–7
### 4. The Trinity and the Person of Christ
Chapters 6 & 14 from *Bible Doctrine*
Scripture Memory—John 1:14
### 5. Providence
Chapter 8 from *Bible Doctrine*
Chapter 8 ("Does Divine Sovereignty Make a Difference in Everyday Life?") from *The Grace of God and the Bondage of the Will* by Jerry Bridges
Scripture Memory—Romans 8:28

## The Doctrine of Man
### 6. Sin
Chapter 1 ("Sin") from *Holiness* by J. C. Ryle

Chapter 5 ("There Is a Lion Outside!") from *A Godward Life, Book II* by John Piper

Chapter 2 ("The Desperateness of Sinners: They Sin Still") from *The Mischief of Sin* by Thomas Watson

Scripture Memory—Jeremiah 17:9

### 7. Pride
"The Cross and Criticism" by Alfred Poirer from *The Journal of Biblical Counseling*

"Pursue the Servant's Mindset" by Stuart Scott from *The Journal of Biblical Counseling*

"The Fifty Fruits of Pride" by Brent Detwiler

Scripture Memory—Philippians 2:3

## The Doctrine of Christ
### 8. Atonement
Chapter 15 from *Bible Doctrine*

Introduction to *The Death of Death in the Death of Christ* by J. I. Packer

Scripture Memory—Romans 3:23–26

### 9. The Gospel
"The Main Thing, Part 1 and II" (CD format) by C. J. Mahaney

"The Gospel: An Evangelical Celebration"

Chapters 1, 2, 5, and 6 from *The Cross Centered Life* by C. J. Mahaney

Scripture Memory—II Timothy 1:13–14

## The Doctrine of the Application of Redemption
### 10. Common Grace/Election
Chapters 17 & 18 from *Bible Doctrine*

Scripture Memory—Ephesians 1:3–6

### 11. The Gospel Call/Regeneration
Chapters 19 & 20 from *Bible Doctrine*

Scripture Memory—Matthew 11:28–30

### 12. Conversion/Justification/Adoption

Chapters 21 & 22 from *Bible Doctrine*

Scripture Memory—Romans 3:27

### 13. Devotion/Passion for God

Preface and Introduction from *A Hunger for God* by John Piper

Chapter 8 ("An Appetite for God") from *Disciplines for Life* by C. J. Mahaney

Scripture Memory—Luke 14:26–27

### 14. Spiritual Disciplines

Chapter 1 ("The Spiritual Disciplines . . . for the Purpose of Godliness") from *Spiritual Disciplines for the Christian Life* by Donald Whitney

"Ten Questions to Ask to Make Sure You're Still Growing" by Donald Whitney from *Discipleship Journal*

Scripture Memory—II Peter 3:18

### 15. Sanctification

"To Take the Soul to Task" by David Powlison from *The Journal of Biblical Counseling*, chapter 3 ("Do We Really Need Help?") & chapter 4 ("The Heart Is the Target") from *Instruments in the Hands of the Redeemer* by Paul Tripp

Scripture Memory—I Timothy 4:7–8

### 16. Sanctification

Chapter 7 ("X-Ray Questions") & chapter 8 ("I Am Motivated When I Feel Desire") from *Seeing with New Eyes* by David Powlison

Scripture Memory—Ephesians 5:25–26

## Leadership

### 17. Marriage

Chapter 2 ("Headship and Authority"), chapter 3 ("The Duties of Husbands and Wives") and chapter 7 ("The Marriage Bed Is Honorable") from *Reforming Marriage* by Doug Wilson

Scripture Memory—Ephesians 6:1–4

### 18. Parenting I

Chapter 1 ("A Short Overview of Covenantal Childrearing") and chapter 3 ("The Duties of Parents Before God") from *Standing on the Promises* by Doug Wilson

Scripture Memory—Proverbs 22:6

### 19. Parenting II

"Gospel Centered Parenting" (CD format) by C. J. Mahaney

"Train Up a Child . . . " (CD format) by Kenneth Maresco

"Train Them Up" (CD format) by Grant Layman

Outline from "Foundations of Child Training" seminar at Covenant Life Church

Scripture Memory—Romans 12:11

### 20. Church

"The Marks of a Spiritual Leader" by John Piper

Scripture Memory—Ephesians 2:8–10

### 21. Motivating by Grace

"The Adventure of God-Centered Leadership" (CD format) by C. J. Mahaney

Scripture Memory—Deuteronomy 6:4–9; Proverbs 1:7; Proverbs 3:5–6

## Evangelism

### 22. Evangelism

"Warn Them" (CD format) by Bob Donohue

Chapter 2 ("Straying through an Infinite Nothing") from *Can Man Live Without God?* by Ravi Zacharias

Scripture Memory—Acts 4:12; Romans 10:9–10; Romans 10:14–15

## 9Marks

### Building Healthy Churches

9Marks exists to equip church leaders with a biblical vision and practical resources for displaying God's glory to the nations through healthy churches.

To that end, we want to see churches characterized by these nine marks of health:

1  Expositional Preaching
2  Biblical Theology
3  A Biblical Understanding of the Gospel
4  A Biblical Understanding of Conversion
5  A Biblical Understanding of Evangelism
6  Biblical Church Membership
7  Biblical Church Discipline
8  Biblical Discipleship
9  Biblical Church Leadership

Find all our Crossway titles
and other resources at
www.9Marks.org